*T*his book is a special gift

*T*o:

Joe

*F*rom:

Marie

*D*ate:

25-12-2003 .

*M*essage:

~~Sarah~~ Isaiah 43.V1-3

Journey of FAITH

Charles R. Swindoll

Christian Art Gifts

JOURNEY OF FAITH
by Charles R. Swindoll

The edition issued by special arrangement with Zondervan
Publishing House, Grand Rapids, Michigan, USA.

Originally published under the title *Come before winter and
share my hope.* Copyright © 1994 by the Zondervan Corporation.

Excerpts taken from *Come before winter.*
Copyright © 1991 by Charles R. Swindoll, Inc.

Unless otherwise indicated, all Scripture quotations are taken
from the *Holy Bible,* New International Version. Copyright ©
1973, 1978, 1984 by International Bible Society. Used by
permission of Zondervan Publishing House. All rights reserved.

The *NIV* and *New International Version* trademarks
are registered in the United States Patent and
Trademark Office by International Bible Society.

© 2000 Christian Art, PO Box 1599,
Vereeniging, 1930, South Africa

Designed by Christian Art

ISBN 1-86852-596-1

Printed in Hong Kong

00 01 02 03 04 05 06 07 08 09 - 10 9 8 7 6 5 4 3 2 1

Journey of FAITH

JANUARY

Begin Anew

*He who was seated on the throne
said, "I am making everything new!"
Then he said, "Write this down, for
these words are trustworthy and true."*
Revelation 21:5

One of the most encouraging things about new years, new weeks, and new days is the word *new*. Friend Webster reveals its meaning: "refreshed, different from one of the same that has existed previously ... unfamiliar." Best of all, a new year is a place to start over. Refresh yourself. Change directions.

JANUARY 2

ON THE FREEWAY OF LIFE

*Listen, my son, and be wise, and keep
your heart on the right path.*
Proverbs 23:19

To start over, you have to know where you
are. *Before you find your way out, you must
determine where you are.* That's true in a de-
partment store or a big church, on a free-
way ... or in *life*. Very, very seldom does
anybody "just happen" to end up on the
right road. The process involved in redi-
recting our lives is often painful, slow, and
even confusing.

STARTING WHERE YOU ARE

*But he was pierced for our transgressions,
he was crushed for our iniquities; the
punishment that brought us peace was
upon him, and by his wounds we are healed.*
Isaiah 53:5

Where are you? Start *there*. Openly and
freely declare your need to the One who
cares deeply. Don't hide a thing. He's ready
to heal every one.

CALL THE SPECIALIST

He heals the broken-hearted
and binds up their wounds.
Psalm 147:3

God is a Specialist at making something useful and beautiful out of something broken and confused.

COME ASIDE AND START ANEW

The promise is for you and your children and for all who are far off – for all whom the Lord our God will call.
Acts 2:39

To help you start anew, personalize the Scripture by praying through Hebrews 10:15-25.

HOPE DURING THE MIDWINTER'S BLAST

*... (And for this we labor and strive),
that we have put our hope in the living
God, who is the Savior of all men,
and especially of those who believe.*
1 Timothy 4:10

Hope doesn't require a massive chain where heavy links of logic hold it together. A thin wire will do ... just strong enough to get us through the night until the winds die down.

STRENGTH IS WEAKNESS

That is why, for Christ's sake, I delight in weaknesses, in insults, in hardships, in persecutions, in difficulties. For when I am weak, then I am strong.
2 Corinthians 12:10

My grace is sufficient for you, for power is perfected in weakness. Most gladly, therefore, I will rather boast about my weakness, that the power of Christ may dwell in me.
2 Corinthians 12:9 (NASB)

JANUARY 8

AN ESSENTIAL COMMODITY

*... let us throw off everything that hinders
and the sin that so easily entangles, and
let us run with perseverance the race
marked out for us ... so that you will
not grow weary and lose heart.*
Hebrews 12:1, 3

The byproduct of hope's sudden break-through is called perseverance ... a rare commodity in today's shallow times. But oh, so essential! It is all you need to take the chill out of the air.

JANUARY 9

A Reservoir Of Power

"I thank and praise you, O God of my fathers:
You have given me wisdom and power, you have
made known to me, what we asked of you, you
have made known to us the dream of the king."
Daniel 2:23

God has somehow placed into the Christian's insides a special something, that extra inner reservoir of power that is more than a match for the stuff life throws at us. When in operation, phenomenal accomplishments are achieved, sometimes even *miraculous*.

LIMITLESS POWER

"I have given you authority to trample on snakes and scorpions, and to overcome all the power of the enemy; nothing will harm you."
Luke 10:19

If you know the Lord, you are the recipient of limitless ability ... His incredible strength.

I can do all things through Him who strengthens me.
Philippians 4:13 (NASB)

Facing The Truth

*"Why do you look at the speck of sawdust
in your brother's eye and pay no attention
to the plank in you own eye? You hypocrite,
first take the plank out of your own eye,
and then you will see clearly to remove
the speck from your brother's eye."*
Matthew 7:3, 5

The sooner we are willing to own up realistically to our responsibility and stop playing the blame game at pity parties for ourselves, the more we'll learn and change and the less we'll burn and blame. Let's face it, we don't because we won't ... we disobey because we want to, not because we have to ... because we choose to, not because we're forced to.

COME ASIDE AND MEMORIZE THIS TRUTH

Because he himself suffered when he was tempted, he is able to help those who are being tempted.
Hebrews 2:18

No temptation has overtaken you but such as is common to man; and God is faithful, who will not allow you to be tempted beyond what you are able, but with the temptation will provide the way of escape also, that you may be able to endure it.
1 Corinthians 10:13 (NASB)

ABOUT EASY SOLUTIONS

Trust in the Lord and do good; dwell in the land and enjoy safe pasture. Delight yourself in the Lord and he will give you the desires of your heart. Commit your way to the Lord; trust in him and he will do this.
Psalm 37:3-5

Henry L. Mencken wrote: There's always an easy solution to every human problem – neat, plausible, and wrong.

Go To The Master

*He got up, rebuked the wind and
said to the waves, "Quiet! Be still!"
Then the wind died down and it was
completely calm. They were terrified
and asked each other, "Who is this?
Even the wind and the waves obey him!"*
Mark 4:39, 41

Jesus is a master at turning devastation
into restoration. His provision is profound,
attainable, and right.

Find Refreshment

The Lord is my shepherd, I shall not be in want. He makes me lie down in green pastures, he leads me beside quiet waters, he restores my soul. He guides me in paths of righteousness for his name's sake.
Psalm 23:1-3

Come to Me, all you who labor and are ... overburdened, and I will cause you to rest – I will ease and relieve and refresh your souls.
Matthew 11:28 (AMP)

COME TO JESUS

*"Take my yoke upon you and learn from me,
for I am gentle and humble in heart, and you
will find rest for your souls. For my yoke is
easy and my burden is light."*
Matthew 11:29-30

When Jesus Christ opens the gate, gently looks at you and says, "Come to Me," what does He mean? He wants you just to *come*. Unload. Unhook the pack and drop it in His lap ... now. Allow Him to take your stress as you take His rest.

DOES ANYONE REALLY UNDERSTAND?

*And being in anguish, he prayed more
earnestly, and his sweat was like drops
of blood falling to the ground.*
Luke 22:44

Does Jesus understand what trauma is all about? Remember, He's the One whose sweat became like drops of blood in the agony of Gethsemane. If anybody understands trauma He does. Completely. Come to Him.

COME ASIDE
AND PROBE

Then the Lord will be jealous for his land
and take pity on his people. The Lord will
reply to them: "I am sending you grain,
new wine and oil, enough to satisfy
you fully; never again will I make
you an object of scorn to the nations."
Joel 2:18-19

Probe closely into God's heart – go ahead,
He won't mind! – as you read His words
to His people in Joel 2:18-32.

JANUARY 19

PERSISTENCE

Then the Lord said to Satan, "Have you considered my servant Job? There is no one on earth like him; he is blameless and upright, a man who fears God and shuns evil. And he still maintains his integrity, though you incited me against him to ruin him without any reason."
Job 2:3

Persistence pays.

A Great Investment

" ... Except Caleb son of Jephunneh.
He will see it, and I will give
him and his descendants the land
he set his feet on, because he
followed the Lord wholeheartedly."
Deuteronomy 1:36

Persistence is a costly investment, no question about it. But the dividends are so much greater than the original outlay that you'll almost forget the price. And if the final benefits are *really* significant, you'll wonder why you ever hesitated to begin with.

TEMPTED TO GIVE UP

Blessed is the man who perseveres under trial, because when he has stood the test, he will receive the crown of life that God has promised to those who love him.
James 1:12

A primary reason we are tempted to give up is other people ... you know, the less than twenty percent whose major role it is in life to persuade others to toss in the towel. For *whatever* reason. Those white-flag specialists never run out of excuses you and I ought to use for quitting. The world's full of "why-sweat-it" experts.

PERSISTENCE PAYS OFF

Never be lacking in zeal, but keep your spiritual fervor, serving the Lord. Be joyful in hope, patient in affliction, faithful in prayer.
Romans 12:11-12

How many military battles would never have been won without persistence? How many men and women would never have graduated from school ... or stayed together in marriage ... or reared a retarded child? How about the great compositions or paintings that would never have been finished? Back behind the impeccable beauty of each work is a dream that wouldn't die mixed with the dogged determination of a gifted genius of whom this indifferent world is not worthy.

JANUARY 23

PARENTS OF CREATIVITY

*A man was there by the name of Zacchaeus; he
was a chief tax collector
and was wealthy. He wanted to see
who Jesus was, but being a short man
he could not, because of the crowd.
So he ran ahead and climbed a
sycamorefig tree to see him, since
Jesus was coming that way. When Jesus reached
the spot, he looked up and said to him,
"Zacchaeus, come down immediately. I must
stay at your house today."*
Luke 19:2-5

If necessity is the mother of invention,
persistence is certainly the father.

Divine Persistence

*"As for the person who hears my
words but does not keep them, I do
not judge him. For I did not come
to judge the world, but to save it."*
John 12:47

God honors persistence. Maybe because
He models it so well. His love for His
people, the Jews, persists to this very day,
even though they have disobeyed Him
more often than they have loved Him in
return. And just think of His patient persistence in continually reaching out to the
lost, "... not wishing for any to perish, but
for all to come to repentance" *(2 Peter 3:9,*
NASB).

CONSTRUCTION UNDERWAY

"He who overcomes will, like them, be dressed in white. I will never blot out his name from the book of life, but will acknowledge his name before my Father and his angels."
Revelation 3:5

He who began a good work in you will continue until the day of Jesus Christ – right up to the time of His return – developing (that good work) and perfecting and bringing it to full completion in you.
Philippians 1:6 (AMP)

SET A GOAL!

I desire to do your will, O my God;
your law is within my heart.
Psalm 40:8

You've got the winter in front of you. Think of these weeks as a time framework for your own investment. Choose an objective carefully, state it clearly in writing, then, with the persistence of an athlete training for the next Olympiad, *go for the goal!*

COME ASIDE AND COMPLETE THE TASK

" ... Do not be afraid of what they say or terrified by them, though they are a rebellious house. You must speak my words to them, whether they listen or fail to listen ... "
Ezekiel 2:6-7

Use Ezekiel's call from the Lord in Ezekiel 2:1-8 to motivate your persistence in completing the tasks God has given you.

Facing A Challenge

Therefore confess your sins to each other and pray for each other so that you may be healed. The prayer of a righteous man is powerful and effective.
James 5:16

Do you need strength? Peace? Wisdom? Direction? Discipline? Ask for it. God will hear you.

Learn From David As He Conquered Goliath: Lesson One

... and I no longer live, but Christ lives in me. The life I live in the body I live by faith in the Son of God, who loved me and gave himself for me.
Galatians 2:20

Prevailing over giants isn't accomplished by using their technique. David's greatest piece of armor, the lethal weapon that made him unique and gave him victory, was his inner *shield of faith*. It kept him free from fear, made him hard of hearing threats, gave him cool composure amidst chaos, it cleared his vision.

LEARN FROM DAVID AS HE CONQUERED GOLIATH: LESSON TWO

*So David triumphed over the
Philistine with a sling and a stone;
without a sword in his hand he struck
down the Philistine and killed him.*
1 Samuel 17:50

*C*onquering giants isn't accomplished without
great skill and discipline. To be God's war-
rior, to fight His way, demands much more
expertise and control than one can imagine. Using the sling and stone of the Spirit
is a far more delicate thing than swinging
the club of the flesh. But oh, how sweet is
the victory when the stone finds its mark
... *and how final.*

WHAT TO DO WHEN YOU FACE A GIANT

And pray in the Spirit on all occasions with all kinds of prayers and requests ...
Ephesians 6:18

Don't run ... but don't try a bigger club, either. Be like David. Turn your Goliath over to Jehovah, the giant-killer. Explain to your powerful God how anxious you are for *Him* to win this victory for a change – not the giant, and not you.

FEBRUARY

THE MOST
OF YOUR TIME

*I thought in my heart, "God will bring
to judgment both the righteous and the
wicked, for there will be a time for
every activity, a time for every deed."*
Ecclesiastes 3:17

The great difference between one person
and another lies largely in his or her use of
time.

USE TIME WISELY

*Be very careful, then, how you live —
not as unwise but as wise, making the
most of every opportunity, because the
days are evil. Therefore do not be foolish,
but understand what the Lord's will is.*
Ephesians 5:15-17

IF ONLY THERE WERE MORE HOURS IN A DAY!

There is a time for everything, and a season for every activity under heaven ...
Ecclesiastes 3:1

Our goal is not to *find more time* but to *use time more wisely*.

THERE IS ENOUGH TIME ... REALLY!

My times are in your hands ...
Psalm 31:15

God has given you (as He gave His Son) sufficient time in each day for you to fulfill His perfect plan – including the interruptions! If you're fudging on your sleep or becoming a frantic, nail-biting, hurried Christian, then you are adding to your day too many things that simply are not His will for you.

COME ASIDE AND APPRAISE YOUR WEEK

... Make the most of every opportunity.
Colossians 4:5

If there are leaks in your time dike, why not plug them?

If your priorities should be sifted more clearly from the trivia, that would be to your advantage.

If a simple plan would help to organize your day, that's only playing it smart.

If you should give a kind but unqualified, unexplained "No" more often, do it.

CONTROLLING OUR TIME

As a result, he does not live the rest of
his earthly life for evil human desires,
but rather for the will of God.
1 Peter 4:2

It's easy to forget that time is our slave,
not our sovereign.

PARTNERSHIP IN TIME MANAGEMENT

You see, at just the right time,
when we were still powerless,
Christ died for the ungodly.
Romans 5:6

God's part ... the timing of my Redeemer.
My part ... the redeeming of my time.

PAIN

... we also rejoice in our sufferings,
because we know that suffering
produces perseverance; perseverance,
character; and character, hope. And
hope does not disappoint us ...
Romans 5:3-5

Pain humbles the proud. It softens the stubborn. It melts the hard.

Preparation Of Pain

*Brothers, as an example of patience in
the face of suffering, take the prophets
who spoke in the name of the Lord.*
James 5:10

I have tried and I cannot find, either in
Scripture or history, a strong-willed
individual whom God used greatly until
He allowed him to be hurt deeply.

COME ASIDE AND PICTURE A PROPHET'S PAIN

"For he did not kill me in the womb,
with my mother as my grave, her
womb enlarged for ever. Why did I
ever come out of the womb to see trouble
and sorrow and to end my days in shame?"
Jeremiah 20:17-18

Jeremiah 20 is a short but vivid picture of a prophet's pain — both inward and outward. Feel your way through this passage. Try to identify with Jeremiah, especially in his highly emotional words of verses 17-18. What can you learn from this hurting man of God?

God Is Molding You

"But he knows the way that I take; when he has tested me, I will come forth as gold."
Job 23:10

Are you at the very brink of despair, thinking that you cannot bear another day of heartache? As difficult as it may be for you to believe this today, the Master knows what He's doing. Your Savior knows your breaking point. The bruising and crushing and melting process is designed to reshape you, *not ruin you*. Your value is increasing the longer He lingers over you.

THE HAMMER, THE FILE, AND THE FURNACE

"This third I will bring into the fire;
I will refine them like silver and test
them like gold. They will call on my
name and I will answer them ... "
Zechariah 13:9

Those whom God uses most effectively have been hammered, filed, and tempered in the furnace of trials and affliction.

Innovation

Do not conform any longer to the pattern of this world, but be transformed by the renewing of your mind. Then you will be able to test and approve what God's will is – his good, pleasing and perfect will.

Romans 12:2

When we innovate, we change, we flex. We approach the standard operating procedure, not like a soft-footed Indian scout sneaking up on a deer by the brook, but rather like Wild Bill Hickok in a saloon with both guns blazing.

Innovation Takes Work

Now when a man works, his wages are not credited to him as a gift, but as an obligation.
Romans 4:4

Michelangelo takes the stand and testifies. These are his actual words: "If people knew how hard I worked to get my mastery, it wouldn't seem so wonderful after all."

ONE, TWO,
THREE – GULP

The Lord preserves the faithful,
but the proud he pays back in full.
Psalm 31:22

Swallowing our pride shouldn't be that difficult, since that's what we eat all day.

TRY IT; YOU'LL LIKE IT!

*Therefore we do not lose heart. Though
outwardly we are wasting away, yet
inwardly we are being renewed day by day.*
2 Corinthians 4:16

Go ahead and give innovation a whirl.
Take one of those many things that keep
dragging you under and search for a creative way to solve the problem. And don't
quit until it's done ... and that smile of
relief will return to your face.

Radical Adjustments

*You were taught, with regard to
your former way of life, to put off
your old self, which is being corrupted
by its deceitful desires; to be made
new in the attitude of your minds ...*
Ephesians 4:22-23

Extreme dilemmas are usually solved by
radical adjustments. It used to be called
"fighting fire with fire." Minor alterations
won't do. If the situation is getting completely out of hand, a slight modification
won't cut it. It's get-with-it time.

A Radical Solution

For he has rescued us from the
dominion of darkness and brought
us into the kingdom of the Son he loves.
Colossians 1:13

Had Christ not taken a drastic step, sinners like us would've never survived the fall. We would never have been rescued. We would be permanently lost. The cross was God's incredible response to our extreme dilemma. Christ did something radical. Now it's your turn.

Radically Practical

"Submit to God and be at peace with him;
in this way prosperity will come to you.
What you decide on will be done, and
light will shine on your ways."
Job 22:21, 28

The most radical alternative may sometimes be the most practical.

COME ASIDE AND TAKE A RADICAL STEP

"Have I not commanded you? Be strong and courageous. Do not be terrified; do not be discouraged, for the Lord your God will be with you wherever you go."
Joshua 1:9

Commit again to the Lord the radical step which you believe He wants you to take. Remember these words from Joshua 1:9 as you do: "Have I not commanded you? Be strong and courageous. Do not be terrified; do not be discouraged, for the Lord your God will be with you wherever you go."

DON'T GARBLE
THAT MESSAGE!

*"True instruction was in his mouth and
nothing false was found on his lips. He
walked with me in peace and uprightness,
and turned many from sin."*
Malachi 2:6

Garbled messages provide the perfect fuel
for gossip sessions and just the right
ingredient for slanderous slams. Exaggerate this detail or rearrange that fact and
you've got a recipe that'll make more
mouths water than hot fudge on a cold
rainy night.

GOD SPEAKS
IN SPECIFICS

"With him I speak face to face,
clearly and not in riddles ... "
Numbers 12:8

God's style of communication doesn't seem to leave much margin for generalities. He told more than one prophet to say it painfully straight and make it obviously clear. He gave Moses precisely ten commandments, not "a dozen or so."

HEAR THE CALL

*Set a guard over my mouth, O Lord;
keep watch over the door of my lips.*
Psalm 141:3

The battle is raging. If ever we needed "a clear call" from the bugler, it is now. Are you responsible for passing on information? Tighten your lips! Hit the right note! *Don't garble that message!*

Come Aside And Grow In Clarity

"In that day," declares the Lord, "I will gather the lame; I will assemble the exiles and those I have brought to grief. I will make the lame a remnant, those driven away a strong nation. The Lord will rule over them in Mount Zion from that day and for ever."
Micah 4:6-7

Observe God's style of communication in the ringing message of Micah 4:1-7, a model of clarity. If there's something you've been trying unsuccessfully to communicate to someone, take time now to write it down as clearly as you can.

Choose Today

*" ... My Father will honor
the one who serves me."*
John 12:26

Now then, revere the Lord, and serve Him in sincerity and truth. Reject the gods which your ancestors served beyond the river and in Egypt, and serve the Lord. However, if it seems wrong in your eyes to serve the Lord, choose today whom you will serve – whether the gods whom your fathers served beyond the river or the gods of the Amorites in whose land you live. Nevertheless, I and my house, we shall serve the Lord.

Joshua 24:14-15 (MLB)

JOSHUA: A GREAT LEADER

... the same Lord is Lord of all and richly blesses all who call on him, for, "Everyone who calls on the name of the Lord will be saved."
Romans 10:12-13

Joshua was a strong leader who knew where he was going, but gave others the space they needed to choose for themselves. No threats. No name-calling. No public put-downs. No exploitation or manipulation or humiliation. He knew what God would have him do, and he realized the consequences of their choosing differently ... but they needed to weigh those issues for themselves.

WHEN MAKING
IMPORTANT DECISIONS

And find out what pleases the Lord.
Ephesians 5:10

If we don't wrestle with the issues on our own, the resulting decision may be superficial ... fragile ... a commitment that may very well melt under the inevitable heat of difficulty and trial.

THINK BEFORE SUBMITTING

"The Lord your God has blessed you in all the work of your hands. He has watched over your journey through this vast desert. These forty years the Lord your God has been with you, and you have not lacked anything."
Deuteronomy 2:7

If mindless submission is the approach you prefer, let me remind you of two words, just two words – *Watergate* and *Jonestown*.

THINK WISELY

*"Why don't you judge for
yourselves what is right?"*
Luke 12:57

In day-to-day living, when issues are not clearly spelled out in Scripture, when there is a lot of gray instead of black and white, we need to: Think wisely. Weigh the alternatives. Choose for ourselves. Decide now.

MARCH

EXPLANATIONS

But Peter and John replied, "Judge for yourselves whether it is right in God's sight to obey you rather than God."
Acts 4:19

All the evils of the world, once black as tar, have turned strange shades of gray. Instead of our seeing them clearly as wrong or someone's fault, they became fuzzy ... and ultimately "explainable." Which being interpreted, means "excusable."

OUR UPSIDE-DOWN WORLD

Who is wise? He will realise these things. Who is discerning? He will understand them. The ways of the Lord are right; the righteous walk in them, but the rebellious stumble in them.
Hosea 14:9

In our society today, it's now the guilty who is more protected than the victim. It's the one who protests an act of violence who is frowned upon, not the doer of the deed. It's the guy who uses words like *discipline* and *diligence* and *integrity* and *blame* and *shame* who is the weirdo, not the one who has developed the scientific gift of explanation and rationalization.

A GOOD TRADE

*"In the same way, let your light shine before
men, that they may see your good deeds
and praise your Father in heaven."*
Matthew 5:16

Seek to replace your explanations with de-
cisions and actions.

DECIDE AND ACT

*Whatever you do, work at it with all
your heart, as working for the Lord ...*
Colossians 3:23

Let's say farewell to foggy terms like: "I
am thinking about it ... " and "Someday I
plan to ... " Let's replace them with: "I have
decided to ... ", "I will no longer ... ", "I
am wrong ... "

JUST DO IT!

"But the one who hears my words and does not put them into practice is like a man who built a house on the ground without a foundation ... "
Luke 6:49

After telling His disciples how to live ful-filled lives, Jesus put the clincher on it by adding, "If you know these things, happy are you if you *do* them."

COME ASIDE
AND TAKE ACTION

Do not merely listen to the word, and so deceive yourselves. Do what it says.
James 1:22

Read with complete openness James 1:22-25. And don't let another day slip by without taking action on that issue about which you know God has been prompting you.

OVERLOOKED
AND UNDERRATED

*A man finds joy in giving an apt reply
– and how good is a timely word!*
Proverbs 15:23

What gets overlooked in the midst of our breakneck schedules? Just a simple word ... *helping.*

HELPING OTHERS

Who comforts us in all our troubles, so that we can comfort those in any trouble with the comfort we ourselves have received from God.
2 Corinthians 1:4

It's about being of assistance ... your arm around the hunched shoulder of another ... your smile saying "try again" to someone who's convinced it's curtains ... your cup of cool water held up to a brother's cracked lips, reassuring and reaffirming.

LOVE AND GOOD DEEDS

Be devoted to one another in brotherly love. Honor one another above yourselves.
Romans 12:10

Let us hold unswervingly to the hope we profess, for he who promised is faithful. And let us consider how we may spur one another on toward love and good deeds.
Hebrews 10:23-24

COME ASIDE AND
HELP SOMEONE

*... so that, having been justified
by his grace, we might become heirs
having the hope of eternal life ... And
I want you to stress these things, so
that those who have trusted in God may
be careful to devote themselves to
doing what is good. These things are
excellent and profitable for everyone.*
Titus 3:7-8

Feed on Titus 3:3-8. Before this time to-morrow, give special help to someone you know.

DENIM DREAMS

... and let us run with perseverance the race marked out for us. Let us fix our eyes on Jesus ...
Hebrews 12:1-2

People who are in great demand today are those who can see something in their imaginations – then pull it off. Those who can think – then follow through. Those who dress their daring dreams in practical denim workclothes. That takes a measure of gift, a pinch of skill, and a ton of discipline!

PRACTICAL DRIVERS

Accept him whose faith is weak, without passing judgment on disputable matters.
Romans 14:1

Being practical requires that we traffic in reality, staying flexible at the intersections where stop-and-go lights flash. It also demands an understanding of others who are driving so as to avoid collisions.

The "Whats" And "Hows" Of Practical Living

A certain ruler asked him, "Good teacher, what must I do to inherit eternal life?"
Luke 18:18

The favorite expressions of a practical soul often begin with "what" or "how." What does the job require? What do you expect of me? How does it work? How long will it take?

An Odd Couple

Live in harmony with one another ...
Romans 12:16

Dreamers don't mix too well with pragmatists. They irritate each other when they rub together ... yet both are necessary. Take away the former and you've got a predictable and occasionally dull result. Remove the latter and you've got creative ideas without wheels, slick visions without handles ... and you go broke trying to get it off the runway.

The Bills
Have To Be Paid

All hard work brings a profit, but mere talk leads only to poverty.
Proverbs 14:23

Dreams are great and visions are fun. But in the final analysis, when the bills come due, they'll be paid by manual labor. *Labor* ... hard work forged in the furnace of practicality.

Come Aside And Learn From Nehemiah

I answered them by saying, "The God of heaven will give us success. We his servants will start rebuilding ... "
Nehemiah 2:20

Get a feel for Nehemiah's good mix of vision and practicality by reading as much as you can in chapters 2, 6, and 13 in his book. What were this man's strengths, and how can you emulate them?

"LITTLE" PEOPLE, "BIG" PEOPLE

The acts of the sinful nature are obvious ... hatred, discord, jealousy, fits of rage, selfish ambition, dissensions, factions and envy ...
Galatians 5:19-20

"Little" people (regardless of their physical size) find it extremely difficult to applaud another's achievement, especially if the accomplishments bear the marks of success and excellence. While there are many who are big enough to appreciate outstanding work, there is always the "little" world comprising those who frown, depreciate, question, doubt, criticize, and forever search for the flaw.

WHEN IT'S RIGHT TO IGNORE

Warn a divisive person once, and then warn him a second time. After that, have nothing to do with him. You may be sure that such a man is warped and sinful; he is self-condemned.
Titus 3:10-11

Ignore the "little" world of onlookers who are too petty to produce, too suspicious to affirm, too envious to acknowledge greatness. Go hard after your goal ... *get on with it!*

Stand Past

*I have fought the good fight,
I have finished the race, I have kept
the faith. Now there is in store for
me the crown of righteousness ...*
2 Timothy 4:7-8

So ... continue to be firm, incapable of being moved, always letting the cup run over ... because you know that your labor in the service of the Lord is never thrown away.
1 Corinthians 15:58 (WILLIAMS)

Aim High

"Even to your old age and grey hairs I am he, I am he who will sustain you. I have made you and I will carry you; I will sustain you and I will rescue you."
Isaiah 46:4

Regardless of your stature, in spite of your current circumstances, age, status, occupation, location, limitations, or background, aim high ... way up there where the ranks are as thin as the air.

Come Aside And Check Your Aim

"I tell you the truth, anyone who has faith in me will do what I have been doing. He will do even greater things than these, because I am going to the Father. And I will do whatever you ask in my name, so that the Son may bring glory to the Father."
John 14:12-13

Is your aim too low? Make any necessary adjustments.

Prophet Sharing

*But they mocked God's
messengers, despised his words
and scoffed at his prophets ...*
2 Chronicles 36:16

If you are a tomorrow-thinker in a world of yesterday-dwellers, take heart. Realize that you must be true to yourself. While you may not be applauded for your warnings, you will be rewarded for your efforts. Just be patient with those who lack your zest and zeal. Say your piece – shout, if you must – but keep in mind that prophets were seldom heeded, rarely thanked, and never popular.

THE COST OF ACHIEVEMENT

Give her the reward she has earned, and let her works bring her praise at the city gate.
Proverbs 31:31

There is not an achievement worth remembering that isn't stained with the blood of diligence and etched with the scars of disappointment.

Disaster In The Making

One who is slack in his work is brother to one who destroys.
Proverbs 18:9

To run, to quit, to escape, even to *hide* solves nothing ... it only postpones a reckoning with reality. It may feel good now, but it's disaster when the bills come due.

STAND STILL ...
STAND STRONG

That is why, for Christ's sake, I delight in
weaknesses, in insults, in hardships, in
persecutions, in difficulties. For when I
am weak, then I am strong.
2 Corinthians 12:10

Are you facing some difficult battle today?
Don't run! Stand still ... and refuse to re-
treat. Look at it as God looks at it and
draw upon His power to hold up under
the blast. Sure, it's tough. Nobody ever said
the Christian life was easy. He offers something better – His own sustaining presence
through any trouble we may encounter.

In The Heat Of The Day

He will sit as a refiner and purifier of
silver; he will purify the Levites and
refine them like gold and silver.
Then the Lord will have men who
will bring offerings in righteousness.
Malachi 3:3

It was Harry S. Truman who said, "If you don't like the heat, get out of the kitchen." I've not met anyone who was able to stay strong without some time in the kitchen. So my advice is a little different from Truman's: If you don't like the heat – stay in the kitchen and learn to handle it!

COME ASIDE AND DO NOT SURRENDER

Fight the good fight of the faith. Take hold of the eternal life to which you were called when you made your good confession in the presence of many witnesses.
1 Timothy 6:12

In whatever battle that bears down on you today, write down five reasons why you should NOT surrender. For inspiration, look at 1 Timothy 6:11-16 and 2 Timothy 4:5-8.

Balance Is Needed

You were bought at a price ...
1 Corinthians 7:23

A measure of efficiency and discipline in life is absolutely healthy and necessary. Being faithful and dedicated to our work is commendable. "Redeeming the time" is biblical. But there is a point where we no longer enjoy ourselves. We can go to strange extremes – extremes that create inner functional disorders which turn us into slaves.

Jealousy

Therefore, rid yourselves of all malice and all deceit, hypocrisy, envy, and slander of every kind.
1 Peter 2:1

Jealousy begins with full hands but is threatened by the loss of its plenty. It is the pain of losing what I have to someone else, in spite of all my efforts to keep it. Bottom line: Jealousy is as cruel as the grave.

THE DESTRUCTION OF JEALOUSY

Finally, brothers, goodbye. Aim for perfection, listen to my appeal, be of one mind, live in peace. And the God of love and peace will be with you.
2 Corinthians 13:11

Jealousy will decimate a friendship, destroy a marriage, nullify unity on a team, and ruin a church. With squint eyes, jealousy will question motives and deplore another's success. It will become severe, suspicious, narrow, negative.

LOVE IS ...

"Of all the commandments, which is the most important?" "The most important one," answered Jesus, "is this: ... Love the Lord your God ... The second is this: Love your neighbor as yourself."
Mark 12:28-31

Love endures long *and* is patient and kind; love never is envious *nor* boils over with jealousy, is not boastful *or* vainglorious, does not display itself haughtily.
1 Corinthians 13:4 (AMP)

APRIL

Fading Past

*For the wisdom of this world
is foolishness in God's sight.*
1 Corinthians 3:19

Conviction is now being viewed as a neurotic tendency. Discipline is considered somewhat sadistic. Determination is, in the minds of the mesmerized masses, that which characterizes a stubborn fool ... a quality not needed and not wanted by those who seek public approval. Without these qualities, however, you have eliminated the challenge that keeps the game of life exciting and rewarding.

No Heartbeat

*Pray for us. We are sure that we have
a clear conscience and desire to live
honorably in every way.*
Hebrews 13:18

Take away conviction, discipline, and determination and you have cut the heart out of real living.

Words To Die By

*See that what you have heard from
the beginning remains in you. If it
does, you also will remain in the Son
and in the Father. And this is what he
promised us – even eternal life.*
1 John 2:24-25

I have fought the good fight, I have finished the race, I have kept the faith. Now there is in store for me the crown of righteousness, which the Lord, the righteous Judge, will award to me on that day – and not only to me, but also to all who have longed for his appearing.
2 Timothy 4:7-8

DETERMINATION

My steps have held to your paths;
my feet have not slipped.
Psalm 17:5

Show me a company that is efficient, progressive, dynamic, and organized – and I'll be willing to guarantee that behind the scenes, somewhere near or at the top of that company is a well-disciplined, determined leader. The same applies to a church or a Christian organization or a school, a home, a bank, or any other enterprise.

Choose Your Course

The men of Ephraim, though armed with bows, turned back on the day of battle.
Psalm 78:9

The history of man is strewn with the litter of nameless people who faced calamity and hardship, suffering and criticism – and gave up. Or – in the words of Psalm 78 – "They turned back." To you who are tempted to turn back ... I urge you instead to stand firm! The benefits of determination far outweigh the alternate course.

Come Aside And Grow In Determination

However, I consider my life worth nothing to me, if only I may finish the race and complete the task the Lord Jesus has given me – the task of testifying to the gospel of God's grace.
Acts 20:24

Confess to God negligence or laziness which His Spirit is revealing to you, and vow to press on. For motivation along the way, uncover the secret of Paul's determination by reading Acts 20:22-24.

Tough Days

Let us not become weary in doing good, for at the proper time we will reap a harvest if we do not give up.
Galatians 6:9

Let us not lose heart (*Galatians 6:9, NASB*). On tough days, you gotta have heart. Don't quit, whatever you do. Persevere. Stand firm. Be strong, resilient, determined to see it through. Ask God to build a protective shield around your heart, stabilizing you.

Tough Days

Therefore, as we have opportunity, let us do good to all people, especially to those who belong to the family of believers.
Galatians 6:10

Let us do good (*Galatians 6:10*, NASB). Our tendency will be anything but that. Instead of good, we will feel like doing evil. Fume. Swear. Scream. Fight. Pout. Get irritated. Burn up all kinds of emotional BTU's. Rather than parading through that shop-worn routine, stay quiet and consciously turn it *all* over to the Lord.

TOUGH DAYS

Finally, let no one cause me trouble, for I bear on my body the marks of Jesus.
Galatians 6:17

Let no one cause you trouble. Superb advice! Refuse to allow anyone (or *anything*) to gain mastery over you. That throne within you belongs only to the Lord Jesus Christ. Stop leasing it out!

Tough Days

*The grace of our Lord Jesus Christ
be with your spirit, brothers ...*
Galatians 6:18

Let grace be with your spirit (*Galatians 6:18*, NASB). Allow the full impact of grace to flow through your thoughts, your attitudes, your responses, your words. Open the gates and let those good things stampede freely across your tough day. You sit on the fence and relax.

LEARN TO LISTEN

"If only you had paid attention to my commands, your peace would have been like a river, your righteousness like the waves of the sea."
Isaiah 48:18

Most of us were born hearing well, but all of us must learn to *listen* well. Listening is a skill, an art that is in need of being cultivated.

NO PLACE FOR ISLANDS

Keep on loving each other as brothers.
Hebrews 13:1

We need each other. You need someone and someone needs you. Isolated islands we're not. To make this thing called life work, we *must* lean and support. And relate and respond. And give and take. And confess and forgive. And reach out and embrace. And release and rely.

LOVE WITH WHEELS

*Above all, love each other deeply,
because love covers over a multitude
of sins. Offer hospitality to one
another without grumbling.*
1 Peter 4:8-9

Be glad for all God is planning for you. Be patient in trouble, and prayerful always. When God's children are in need, you be the one to help them out. And get into the habit of inviting guests home for dinner or, if they need lodging, for the night.
Romans 12:12-13 (TLB)

LET'S LINK UP!

*Now to each one the manifestation of the
Spirit is given for the common good.*
1 Corinthians 12:7

Since none of us is a whole, independent,
self-sufficient, supercapable, all-powerful
hotshot, let's quit acting like we are. Life's
lonely enough without our playing that
silly role.

COME ASIDE
AND GROW IN LOVE

We who are strong ought to bear with the failings of the weak and not to please ourselves. Each of us should please his neighbor for his good, to build him up.
Romans 15:1-2

Read Romans 15:1-7. Who needs your help today – your understanding, your encouragement, your acceptance?

A GOOD ROLE MODEL

*I answered them by saying, "The God
of heaven will give us success ... "*
Nehemiah 2:20

Looking for a role model on how to handle criticism? Check out the book of Nehemiah. On several occasions this greathearted statesman was openly criticized, falsely accused, and grossly misunderstood. Each time he kept his cool ... he rolled with the punch ... he considered the source ... he refused to get discouraged ... he went to God in prayer ∴ he kept building the wall.
(Nehemiah 2:19-20; 4:1-5)

Do Not Bail Out

*" ... Do not be afraid. Stand firm
and you will see the deliverance the
Lord will bring you today ... "*
Exodus 14:13

One of the occupational hazards of being a leader is receiving criticism (not all of it *constructive*, by the way). In the face of that kind of heat, there's a strong temptation to "throw in the towel." I firmly believe that the leader who does *anything* that is different or worthwhile or visionary can count on criticism.

The Checkered Path Of Victory

*We have come to share in Christ
if we hold firmly till the end the
confidence we had at first.*
Hebrews 3:14

It was Theodore Roosevelt who said, "Far better is it to dare mighty things, to win glorious triumphs even though checkered by failure, than to rank with those poor spirits who neither enjoy nor suffer much because they live in the gray twilight that knows neither victory nor defeat." Keep on daring mighty things.

A Critical Test

*You were bought at a price; do
not become slaves of men.*
1 Corinthians 7:23

Rejoice in the Lord always ...
Philippians 4:4

A sense of humor is of paramount
importance to the leader. Many of God's
servants are simply too serious! There are
at least two tests we face that determine
the extent of our sense of humor: the ability to laugh at ourselves and the ability to
handle criticism.

TAKING CRITICISM

Brothers, stop thinking like children ...
1 Corinthians 14:20

We are foolish if we respond angrily to *every* criticism. Who knows, God may be using those words to teach us some essential lessons, painful though they may be.

LOVING WOUNDS

*Do not rebuke an older man harshly,
but exhort him as if he were your father.
Treat younger men as brothers, older
women as mothers, and younger
women as sisters, with absolute purity.*
1 Timothy 5:1-2

Better is open rebuke than love that is concealed. Faithful are the wounds of a friend, but deceitful are the kisses of an enemy.
Proverbs 27:5-6 (NASB)

A Friend Indeed

*The goal of this command is love,
which comes from a pure heart
and a good conscience and a sincere
faith. Some have wandered away from
these and turned to meaningless talk.*
1 Timothy 1:5-6

Friendship is not threatened but strengthened by honest criticism. But when you are criticized by one who hardly knows you, filter out what is fact ... and ignore the rest!

LET IT FLOW

The words of a man's mouth are deep waters, but the fountain of wisdom is a bubbling brook.
Proverbs 18:4

The river of love must be kept within its banks. Truth on one side, discernment on the other. Otherwise, love will flood indiscriminately and create a disaster.

Come Aside And
Grow In Comfort

*... so that we can comfort those in
any trouble ... If we are distressed, it
is for your comfort and salvation ...
... But this happened that we might
not rely on ourselves but on God ...*
2 Corinthians 1:4, 6, 9

Read 2 Corinthians 1:3-11. In this passage there are at least three reasons for suffering – each one introduced with the term "that." Allow these truths to lead you to praise God today.

BRUISES ATTRACT ONE ANOTHER

If one part suffers, every part suffers with it; if one part is honored, every part rejoices with it.
1 Corinthians 12:26

God allows suffering so that we might have the capacity to enter into others' sorrow and affliction. God gives His children the capacity to understand by bringing similar sufferings into our lives.

DEPEND ON HIM

*That is why I am suffering as I am.
Yet I am not ashamed, because I know
whom I have believed, and am convinced that he is able to guard what
I have entrusted to him for that day.*
2 Timothy 1:12

God allows suffering so that we might
learn what it means to depend on Him,
not on our own strength and resources. It
forces us to lean on Him totally, absolutely.
Over and over He reminds us of the dan-
ger of pride ... but it frequently takes
suffering to make the lesson stick.

THANK YOU

Give thanks in all circumstances, for this is God's will for you in Christ Jesus.
1 Thessalonians 5:18

One of the reasons our suffering is prolonged is that we take so long saying "Thank you, Lord" with an attitude of genuine appreciation. Honestly – have you said, "Thanks, Lord, for this test"? Have you finally stopped struggling and expressed to Him how much you appreciate His loving sovereignty over your life?

THE REFINER'S FIRE

... gold, which perishes even though refined by fire – may be proved genuine ...
1 Peter 1:7

How unfinished and rebellious, proud and unconcerned we would be without suffering!

Relevance

For the word of God is living and active. Sharper than any double-edged sword, it penetrates even to dividing soul and spirit, joints and marrow ...
Hebrews 4:12

Martin Luther on relevance: "If you preach the gospel in all aspects with the exception of the issues which deal specifically with your time – you are not preaching the gospel at all." Don't misunderstand, he wasn't advocating a "social gospel," but rather a word from God that contains the solid ring of relevance.

Some Things
Never Change

"And if anyone takes words away from this book of prophecy, God will take away from him his share in the tree of life and in the holy city, which are described in this book."
Revelation 22:19

The gospel isn't to be changed. It is not ours to tamper with. But it *is* to cut into each generation like a flashing sword, sharpened on the stone of Scripture, tempered in the furnace of reality and need.

MAY

No Room For Boasting

*Ask of me, and I will make the
nations your inheritance, the ends
of the earth your possession.*
Psalm 2:8

For who regards you as superior? And
what do you have that you did not receive?
But if you did receive it, why do you boast
as if you had not received it?
1 Corinthians 4:7 (NASB)

SIMPLE ADVICE

*"We have heard of Moab's pride — her
overweening pride and conceit, her pride
and her insolence — but her boasts are empty."*
Isaiah 16:6

Pride will eat you up. "Just be what ya'
are."

Solomon's Advice

*A man's pride brings him low, but
a man of lowly spirit gains honor.*
Proverbs 29:23

Let another praise you, and not your own
mouth; a stranger, and not your own lips.
Proverbs 27:2 (NASB)

Self-Control

*As you know, we consider blessed those
who have persevered. You have heard
of Job's perseverance and have seen
what the Lord finally brought about ...*
James 5:11

The overindulgence and underachieve-
ment of our age have created a monster
whose brain is lazy, vision is blurred, hands
are greedy, skin is thin, middle is round,
and seat is wide. This does not need to be
us! Under the operation of the Spirit of God,
we have the inner strength to resist and
refrain, the strength *not* to indulge, *not* to
act on impulse.

WHAT ARE YOU PRODUCING?

Do not conform any longer to the pattern of this world, but be transformed by the renewing of your mind. Then you will be able to test and approve what God's will is – his good, pleasing and perfect will.
Romans 12:2

We are the product of what we think about. Our actions and our reactions originate in our minds. What do you think about? Upon what do you spend most of your mental energy? How much independent, hard-core, no-nonsense, controlled mental input goes into your average day?

COME ASIDE AND DRAW ON THE LORD'S STRENGTH

You, however, are controlled not
by the sinful nature but by the Spirit,
if the Spirit of God lives in you ...
Romans 8:9

Don't fail to draw on the Lord's power as you work on self-control, knowing His strength is yours. Understand and believe. Read Romans 8:9-14.

Slow Down!

*"Come to me, all you who are weary
and burdened, and I will give you rest.
Take my yoke upon you and learn from
me, for I am gentle and humble in heart,
and you will find rest for your souls."*
Matthew 11:28-29

Be still, and know that I am God.
Psalm 46:10

PLEASE PRAY!

*Dear children, let us not love with words
or tongue but with actions and in truth.*
1 John 3:18

When you reply to a request for prayer
with, "Yes, I'll pray for you" – do you?

KEEPING YOUR WORD

*Therefore each of you must put
off falsehood and speak
truthfully to his neighbor ...*
Ephesians 4:25

And whatever you do, whether in word
or deed, do it all in the name of the Lord
Jesus.
Colossians 3:17

A Proverb About
Joy And Sorrow

*Carry each other's burdens, and in this
way you will fulfill the law of Christ.*
Galatians 6:2

Shared joy is a double joy, shared sorrow
is half a sorrow.

A Piece In The Divine Puzzle

Now to each one the manifestation of the Spirit is given for the common good.
1 Corinthians 12:7

We need each other. More profoundly, more desperately than we even begin to realize. As a matter of fact, we were given to one another by the Lord of the body – because each one of us has a unique something to contribute – a piece of the divine puzzle no one else on earth can supply.

WE'RE IN THIS TOGETHER

*And one standing alone can be attacked
and defeated, but two can stand back-to-
back and conquer; three is even better.*
Ecclesiastes 4:12 (TLB)

Two can accomplish more than twice as
much as one, for the results can be much
better. If one falls, the other pulls him up;
but if a man falls when he is alone, he's in
trouble.

The Light Of Hope

*"In him was life, and that life was the light
of men. The light shines in the darkness,
but the darkness has not understood it."*
John 1:4-5

There is nothing like light, however small
and distant, to put us on tiptoes in the
darkness.

Discoveries

*But whatever was to my profit I now
consider loss for the sake of Christ.*
Philippians 3:7

There are few joys like the joy of sudden discovery. Instantly forgotten is the pain and expense of the search, the inconveniences, the hours, the sacrifices. Bathed in the ecstasy of discovery, time stands still. Nothing else seems half so important. Lost in the thrill of the moment, we relish the inexpressible finding.

COME ASIDE
AND DISCOVER

*This is what the Lord Almighty
says: "I will save my people from
the countries of the east and the
west." This is what the Lord Almighty
says: ... "Let your hands be strong ..."*
Zechariah 8:7, 9

Delve into the riches of Zechariah 8 – or
choose another passage you haven't been
too familiar with – and write down all the
new discoveries you make. Take your time
– both to search and to savor what you
find.

Gold Mine

*"Ask and it will be given to you;
seek and you will find; knock and
the door will be opened to you."*
Matthew 7:7

Hidden in the Scriptures are priceless verbal vaults. Silent. Hard to find. Easy to miss if you're in a hurry. But they are there, awaiting discovery. God's Word, like a deep, deep mine, stands ready to yield its treasures.

GOD TRANSFORMS
OUR PAST

*Therefore, if anyone is in Christ,
he is a new creation; the old
has gone, the new has come!*
2 Corinthians 5:17

God is the One who builds trophies from
the scrap pile ... who draws His clay from
under the bridge ... who makes clean in-
struments of beauty from the filthy failures of yesteryear.

God Forgives Our Past

*He himself bore our sins in his
body on the tree, so that we might
die to sins and live for righteousness;
by his wounds you have been healed.*
1 Peter 2:24

Looking for sinners, God found us in desperate straits. Lifting us to the level of His much-loved Son, He brought us in, washed our wounds, and changed our direction.

PULLED FROM THE PIT

*For it is by grace you have been saved,
through faith – and this is not from
yourselves, it is the gift of God ...*
Ephesians 2:8

All our church-going and hymn-singing
and long-praying and committee-sitting
and religious-talking will never ease the
fact that we were dug from a deep, dark,
deadly pit. And may we *never* forget it. It
is God's gracious love that pulled us from
that pit.

Going ... Not Knowing

And now, compelled by the Spirit, I am going to Jerusalem, not knowing what will happen to me there.
Acts 20:22

Paul made this statement as he was saying goodbye to a group of friends. What an honest admission! *I am going ... not knowing what will happen ...* That's what this thing called the Christian life is all about, isn't it? Going ... yet not knowing.

WE WILL FOLLOW!

Then a teacher of the law came to him and said, "Teacher, I will follow you wherever you go." Jesus replied, "Foxes have holes and birds of the air have nests, but the Son of Man has no place to lay his head."
Matthew 8:19-20

As followers of our Lord we believe He leads us in a certain direction ... or in pursuit of a precise goal. That leading is unmistakably clear. Not necessarily logical or explainable, but clear. At least *to us!* So — out of sheer obedience — we go. How strange ... yet how typical!

JOURNEY OF FAITH

*"... If anyone would come after
me, he must deny himself and
take up his cross and follow me."*
Mark 8:34

It is no easy thing to leave a sure thing,
walk away from an ace in the hole, and
start down a long, dark tunnel with no
end in sight. Absolutely frightening ... yet
filled with unimaginable excitement.
Going ... yet not knowing. Obeying ... yet
not understanding.

LEAP OF FAITH

By faith Abraham, when called to go to a place he would later receive as his inheritance, obeyed and went, even though he did not know where he was going.
Hebrews 11:8

Is the Lord suggesting it's time for you to take a drastic leap of faith? Before you jump, be sure of four things: Be sure it's the Lord who is speaking. Be sure the decision doesn't contradict Scripture. Be sure your motive is unselfish and pure. Be sure the "leap" won't injure others or your own testimony.

COME ASIDE AND
SING WITH MOSES

*"In your unfailing love you will lead the
people you have redeemed. In your strength
you will guide them to your holy dwelling."*
Exodus 15:13

Moses sang these words a full forty years
before any of the people would dwell in
the Promised Land. Does your faith in
God's loving guidance match this?

PEOPLE ON THE MOVE

"We are aliens and strangers in your sight, as were all our forefathers. Our days on earth are like a shadow, without hope."
1 Chronicles 29:15

God calls us strangers and pilgrims during our short stint on planet Earth. People on the move, living in tents, free and unencumbered, loose and available, ready to roll, willing to break the mold – whenever and wherever He leads. Regardless.

Products Of Our Own Thoughts

For as he thinks within himself,
so he is. He says to you, "Eat and drink!"
But his heart is not with you.
Proverbs 23:7 (NASB)

Our thoughts form the thermostat which regulates what we accomplish in life.

THOUGHTS

"O Lord, God of our fathers Abraham,
Isaac and Israel, keep this desire
in the hearts of your people forever,
and keep their hearts loyal to you."
1 Chronicles 29:18

Thoughts, positive or negative, grow stronger when fertilized with constant repetition. That may explain why so many who are gloomy and gray stay in that mood, and why others who are cheery and enthusiastic continue to be so, even in the midst of difficult circumstances.

DWELL ON
THESE THINGS

*... we take captive every thought to
make it obedient to Christ.*
2 Corinthians 10:5

Finally, brothers, whatever is true, whatever is noble, whatever is right, whatever is pure, whatever is lovely, whatever is admirable ... think about such things.
Philippians 4:8

INPUT, OUTPUT

*"The good man brings good things out of
the good stored up in his heart, and the
evil man brings evil things … "*
Luke 6:45

Our performance in life is directly related
to the thoughts we deposit in our memory
bank. We can only draw on what we have
already deposited.

COME ASIDE AND
BE POSITIVE

*"Yours, O Lord, is the greatness and the
power and the glory and the majesty and the
splendor, for everything in heaven and earth
is yours. Yours, O Lord, is the kingdom; you
are exalted as head over all."*
1 Chronicles 29:11

Put positive vision in your mental tank by
meditating – in the power of the Holy
Spirit – on David's prayer in 1 Chronicles
29:10-13.

WORDS THAT BUILD UP

*The words of the wicked lie in
wait for blood, but the speech
of the upright rescues them.*
Proverbs 12:6

Do not let any unwholesome talk come
out of your mouths, but only what is help-
ful for building others up according to their
needs, that it may benefit those who listen.
Ephesians 4:29

Write this verse on a small card and place
it beside your telephone.

JUNE

Your Speech

*Words from a wise man's
mouth are gracious ...*
Ecclesiastes 10:12

Looking for ways to make your witness more gracious, more winsome? Interested in communicating Christ's love and in building bridges that attract others to Him? Start with your speech.

Seasoned With Salt

*A wise man's heart guides his mouth,
and his lips promote instruction.*
Proverbs 16:23

Let your speech always be with grace, seasoned, as it were, with salt, so that you may know how you should respond to each person.
Colossians 4:6 (NASB)

On Being Real

*May integrity and uprightness protect
me, because my hope is in you.*
Psalm 25:21

To "find yourself" requires that you take
time to look. It's essential if you want to
be a whole person, real to the core. There
are times in all our lives when we need to
back away, slow down, stay quiet, think
through, be still.

BECOMING WHOLE

... goodwill is found among the upright.
Proverbs 14:9

There *has* to be more to life than just do-ing. There is! It's *being*. Becoming whole ... believable ... purposeful ... lovable. The word is *real*. It takes two ingredients to make us real: time and pain.

Take A Look At You

"I am sending you out like sheep
among wolves. Therefore be as shrewd
as snakes and as innocent as doves."
Matthew 10:16

Going through a lot of activities? In a hurry most of the time? Seldom pausing to ask why? Still substituting *doing* for *being?* It will never satisfy. What does God suggest? Having a heart of compassion, being kind, tender, transparent, gentle, patient, forgiving, loving, and lovable. All those things spell R-E-A-L.

COME ASIDE AND GROW IN REALITY

But Ruth replied, "Don't urge me to leave you or to turn back from you. Where you go I will go, and where you stay I will stay. Your people will be my people and your God my God."
Ruth 1:16

Read as much as you have time for in the short book of Ruth, and notice how closely this tender woman embraced life and love. Ruth was real. What can you learn from her?

SOMEDAY

But Timothy has just now come to us from you and has brought good news about your faith and love. He has told us that you always have pleasant memories of us and that you long to see us, just as we also long to see you.
1 Thessalonians 3:6

Someday when the kids are grown, things are going to be a lot different. One by one they'll leave our nest, and the place will begin to resemble order. The house will be quiet ... and calm ... and always clean ... and filled with memories ... and lonely ... and we won't like that at all. And we'll spend our time not looking forward to *someday* but looking back to *yesterday*.

CONTENTMENT

Be joyful always ... give thanks
in all circumstances, for this is God's
will for you in Christ Jesus.
1 Thessalonians 5:16, 18

I have learned to be content in whatever circumstances I am.
Philippians 4:11 (NASB)

SUCCESS IS OVERRATED

*Not that I have already obtained all
this, or have already been made perfect,
but I press on to take hold of that for
which Christ Jesus took hold of me.*
Philippians 3:12

All of us crave success despite daily proof
that man's real genius lies in quite the
opposite direction. It's really incompetence
that we're all pros at. How come we're so
surprised when we see it in others and so
devastated when it has occurred in ourselves? It happens to every one of us. We
all make mistakes ... doing the wrong
thing, usually with the best of motives. Success is actually a journey, not a destina-
tion.

PERFECTIONISM

But we have this treasure in jars of clay to show that this all-surpassing power is from God and not from us.
2 Corinthians 4:7

Show me the guy who wrote the rules for perfectionism and I'll guarantee he's a nailbiter with a face full of tics ... whose wife dreads to see him come home. Furthermore, he forfeits the right to be respected because he's either guilty of not admitting he blew it or he has become an expert at cover-up.

Ease Off

Then Peter ... asked, "Lord, how many times shall I forgive my brother when he sins against me? Up to seven times?" Jesus answered, "I tell you, not seven times, but seventy-seven times."
Matthew 18:21-22

If our perfect Lord is gracious enough to take our worst, our ugliest, our most boring, our least successful, and forgive them, burying them in the depths of the sea, then it's high time we give each other a break.

A Common Bond

We all stumble in many ways ...
James 3:2

Imperfection is one of the few things we still have in common. It links us close together in the same family!

COME ASIDE WHEN
WE BLOW IT

*"... Can a blind man lead a blind man?
Will they not both fall into a pit? A
student is not above his teacher, but everyone
who is fully trained will be like his teacher."*
Luke 6:39-40

What's the significance of Luke 6:37-42
in a world where blowing it is par for the
course?

You Can't Take It With You

But the day of the Lord will come like a thief, and then the heavens will vanish (pass away) with a thunderous crash, and the (material) elements (of the universe) will be dissolved with fire, and the earth and the works that are upon it will be burned up. Since all these things are thus in the process of being dissolved, what kind of person ought (each of) you to be (in the meanwhile) in consecrated and holy behavior and devout and godly qualities ...

2 Peter 3:10-11 (NASB)

KEEP LIFE SIMPLE

*Therefore each of you must
put off falsehood and speak
truthfully to his neighbor, for we
are all members of one body.*
Ephesians 4:25

Want to know how to keep life simple,
fresh as a spring morning? Tell the truth,
the whole truth, and nothing but the truth.

The Church

Surely goodness and love will follow me all the days of my life, and I will dwell in the house of the Lord forever.
Psalm 23:6

Jesus gave an unconditional promise that the church is His personal project ("I will build my church") and also that it will be perpetually invincible. No way will "the gates of hell" put it out of business. When you chew on that thought long enough, you begin to realize that the church is the impervious anvil.

TRUE COMMUNITY

*There are different kinds of
gifts, but the same Spirit.*
1 Corinthians 12:4

It is in the church where people really care.
Not because of status or money. But because the Spirit of God is at work, weaving together the lives within the Body.

Every Sunday

*And God blessed the seventh day and
made it holy, because on it he rested from
all the work of creating that he had done.*
Genesis 2:3

Sunday ... that's when the Body and the
Head meet to celebrate this mysterious
union ... when ordinary, garden-variety
folks like us gather around the pre-eminent
One. For worship. For encouragement. For
instruction. For expression. For support.
For the carrying out of a God-given role
that will never be matched or surpassed
on earth – even though it's the stuff the
world around us considers weird and weak.

AM I MY BROTHER'S KEEPER?

Therefore, if what I eat causes my brother to fall into sin, I will never eat meat again, so that I will not cause him to fall.
1 Corinthians 8:13

When you don't concern yourself with being your brother's keeper, you don't have to get dirty anymore or take risks or lose your objectivity or run up against the thorny side of an issue that lacks easy answers.

COMPASSION

... all of you, live in harmony with one another; be sympathetic, love as brothers, be compassionate and humble.
1 Peter 3:8

How long will it be before we realize that others won't care how much we know until they know how much we care? If you really want to be blessed, prefer compassion to information. We need both, but in the right order.

Come Aside And Hear
Of God's Compassion

*"... I will turn their mourning
into gladness; I will give them
comfort and joy instead of sorrow."*
Jeremiah 31:13

Turn to another prophet and hear the echoes of God's compassion for His people in Jeremiah 31:7-20. Who needs to see this kind of God through *your* life?

SAY IT WELL

"... Those who honor me I will honor, but those who despise me will be disdained."
1 Samuel 2:30

If you preach or teach remember to: study hard, pray like mad, think it through, tell the truth, then stand tall. But while you're on your feet, don't clothe the riches of Christ in rags. Say it well.

THE DAVID-AND-GOLIATH PRINCIPLE

"... The Lord who delivered me from the paw of the lion and the paw of the bear will deliver me from the hand of this Philistine."
1 Samuel 17:37

Empty philosophy doesn't stand a chance against biblical theology. It's the timeless David-and-Goliath principle – one plus God ... aw, you know the equation.

GOD IS NEAR

"... And surely I am with you always,
to the very end of the age."
Matthew 28:20

He is not far from each one of us; for in Him we live and move and exist.
Acts 17:27-28 (NASB)

Come Aside And Grow In Communication

Look for some high-quality communication from Paul in Acts 13:16-41 where he addresses a mixed audience in a synagogue on his first missionary journey.

Too Much

*"The Lord will fight for you;
you need only to be still."*
Exodus 14:14

You've heard of "too little and too late." How about "too many and too much"? Too much empty talk. Too much comparison and commercialism. Too many meetings. Too many options on stuff like cars, sound systems, computers, and soft drinks. Whatever happened to a quiet, barefoot walk along a beach? Or an evening of just listening to music?

First-Class Class

*May integrity and uprightness
protect me, because my hope is in you.*
Psalm 25:21

How nice to be surprised by subtlety. To stumble across genuine beauty, true sincerity without overt attempts to impress. First-class *class* ... understated elegance that leaves room to imagine, to think, to decide for ourselves, to appreciate.

LESS CAN BE MORE

*... we take captive every thought
to make it obedient to Christ.*
2 Corinthians 10:5

How about more originals, fewer copies.
More creativity, less technology. More
implying, less explaining. More thought,
less talk.

Understatements

"The good man brings good things
out of the good stored up in his heart,
and the evil man brings evil things
out of the evil stored up in his heart."
Luke 6:45

"To state with restraint ... for greater effect." That's what understatement means. As in "I love you." Next time you're tempted to gush all over another, just say that.

COME ASIDE

And the words of the Lord are flawless, like silver refined in a furnace of clay, purified seven times.
Psalm 12:6

Read Psalm 12 (which exposes some ungodly overstatement) and notice especially the vivid picture in verse 6. What can you learn from this verse about the process that produces speech that is pure and free from overstatement? And how can you put that process to work today?

JULY

A Lesson From Solomon: Order Your Way

By wisdom a house is built, and through understanding it is established; through knowledge its rooms are filled with rare and beautiful treasures.
Proverbs 24:3-4

In Proverbs 16:1 Solomon admits that "orderly thinking" (MLB) is unique to humanity. He tells us that being mentally organized is not an impossibility. Point: we are built with the ability to think and plan things out.

A Lesson From Solomon: Desire

The sluggard craves and gets nothing, but the desires of the diligent are fully satisfied.
Proverbs 13:4

In Proverbs 13:4 Solomon reminds us that the *desire* to carry out our plans is built in ... even "the sluggard" desires it. Stop and think about yourself. When you're late, you usually have had the desire to be on time. When you fail, you desire to succeed. The internal equipment is fully furnished by our Heavenly Father.

A Lesson From Solomon: Count On God

Commit to the Lord whatever you do, and your plans will succeed.
Proverbs 16:3

God has a perfect will for our lives. He has the ability to "pull things off" in our lives. His timing is perfect. We must depend and count on Him!

ACCOMPLISHING
OUR OBJECTIVES

*The end of a matter is better
than its beginning, and
patience is better than pride.*
Ecclesiastes 7:8

Reasons we don't accomplish our objectives: We have set goals that are unwise and/or unrealistic. We have made plans contradicting God's will. We have failed to get around to it.

THE WORK OF
OUR HANDS

*"Strengthen the feeble hands, steady
the knees that give way."*
Isaiah 35:3

May the favor of the Lord our God rest
upon us; establish the work of our hands
for us – yes, establish the work of our hands.
Psalm 90:17

COME ASIDE AND SEEK HIS WILL

*Come near to God and he
will come near to you ...*
James 4:8

Take some time to look at your life this week. Go before God and give Him your list of objectives, asking Him for His green light ... then with your desire in gear, tighten your belt and get on with it.

LEARNING FROM GRANDPARENTS

"... Is not life more important than food, and the body more important than clothes?"
Matthew 6:25

Grandparents' favorite gesture is open arms and their favorite question is "What do you wanna do?" Their favorite words are "I love you, honey." They don't look for mistakes and failures; they forgive them. They don't skip pages when they read to you. When you want to talk, they want to listen. It's funny, but you somehow get the impression that things like money and possessions and clothes aren't nearly as important as *you*.

STRENGTH IN GODLY GRANDPARENTS

Train a child in the way he should go, and when he is old he will not turn from it.
Proverbs 22:6

Grandparents have made enough errors to understand that perfectionism is a harsh taskmaster and that self-imposed guilt is a hardened killer. They could be superb instructors, but their best lessons are caught, not taught. Their Christianity is seasoned, filtered through the tight weave of realism, heartache, loss, and compromise.

WHAT REALLY MATTERS IN LIFE?

*A wise son brings joy to his father,
but a foolish son grief to his mother.*
Proverbs 10:1

The aging leader, General Douglas MacArthur, in a piece entitled "A Father's Prayer," asks God to build him a son of strong character, humble spirit, a person of compassion, determination, simplicity, greatness. After claiming all these things by faith, he adds: "Then I, his father, will dare to whisper, 'I have not lived in vain.'"

Appearances Can Be Deceiving

"Since you have kept my command to endure patiently, I will also keep you from the hour of trial that is going to come upon the whole world to test those who live on the earth."
Revelation 3:10

Our Lord never wastes times of testing. The pain and struggles and confusion connected with our circumstances only *seem* futile and unfair.

To Know Him Is
To Be Like Him

*(For my determined purpose is) that I may know
Him (that I may progressively become more deeply
and intimately acquainted with Him, perceiving
and recognizing and understanding the wonders
of His Person more strongly and more clearly),
and that I may so share His sufferings as to be
continually transformed (in spirit into His
likeness even) to His death, (in the hope).*
Philippians 3:10 (AMP)

Come Aside And Let God Lead You

... In my distress I called to the Lord, and he answered me. From the depths of the grave I called for help, and you listened to my cry.
Jonah 2:2

Out of the damp darkness, hear in Jonah 2:1-9 the words of a man at a most unique turning point. How would you describe Jonah's new awareness?

THE PROBLEM WITH PROGRESS

And I saw that all labor and all achievement spring from man's envy ...
Ecclesiastes 4:4

Are you an eagle-type, soaring to heights beyond your peers? Don't expect pats on the back or explosions of applause. Mavericks who don't color within the lines are also notorious for not staying within the fences. Many an alleged heretic today will be a hero tomorrow. Which is another way of saying, "first the cross, then the crown."

Enthusiasm

Rejoice in the Lord always.
I will say it again: Rejoice!
Philippians 4:4

In many ways, enthusiasm is the key ingredient that frees us from the cramping, dark, overheated confinement of a task.

EMERSON'S MOTTO

*The warden paid no attention to
anything under Joseph's care, because
the Lord was with Joseph and gave
him success in whatever he did.*
Genesis 39:23

"Nothing great was ever achieved without enthusiasm."

God's Promises:
Fuel For The Fire

*But in keeping with his promise we are
looking forward to a new heaven and a
new earth, the home of righteousness.*
2 Peter 3:13

I'm convinced that one of the reasons God
gives us so many personal promises in His
Word is to stir up our enthusiasm – to build
a bonfire in the steamroom of our souls.

WITHOUT ENTHUSIASM

*"But seek first his kingdom and
his righteousness, and all these
things will be given to you as well."*
Matthew 6:33

Knowledge without enthusiasm is like a bed without sheets ... a "thank you" without a smile. Remove enthusiasm from a church service on Sunday and you have the makings of a memorial service at a mortuary on a Monday. Remove enthusiasm from the daily whirl of family activities and you've made a grinding mill out of a merry-go-round.

The Gift Of Family

*Unless the Lord builds the house,
they labor in vain who build it; unless
the Lord guards the city, the watchman
keeps awake in vain. Behold, children
are a gift of the Lord; the fruit of the
womb is a reward. How blessed is the
man whose quiver is full of them;
they shall not be ashamed, when they
speak with their enemies in the gate.*
Psalm 127:1, 3, 5 (NASB)

REFLECT ON
YOUR FAMILY

God sets the lonely in families.
Psalm 68:6

Is the Lord really building your home?
Stop and think. Do you view the kiddos
as His gift, His reward? Gifts and rewards
in life are usually treated with special care,
you know. Are you genuinely happy with
your full quiver? Is it pleasant for the family
to be with you?

Come Aside And Build Family Memories

Your wife will be like a fruitful vine within your house; your sons will be like olive shoots around your table. Thus is the man blessed who fears the Lord.
Psalm 128:3-4

Get reacquainted with those folks who live under your roof and eat at your table and bear your name ... and prefer you to *any* substitute. Start this week. How about *tonight?* Treat yourself to Psalm 128, as well as a special time with your family.

On Bearing Fruit

"If a man remains in me and I in him,
he will bear much fruit ..."
John 15:5

Lord, since you can "look into the seeds of time, and say which grain will grow, and which will not, speak then to me ..."
Macbeth, I.1

TACT

*What do you prefer? Shall I
come to you with a whip, or
in love and with a gentle spirit?*
1 Corinthians 4:21

Wisely labeled "the saving virtue," tact graces a life like fragrance graces a rose. One whiff of those red petals erases any memory of the thorns. Tact is like that.

A RARE COMMODITY

From the fruit of his lips a man is filled with good things as surely as the work of his hands rewards him.
Proverbs 12:14

Tact is *savior faire* on the horizontal plane. It is incessantly appropriate, invariably attractive, incurably appealing, but rare ... oh, so rare! Its basic function is a keen sense of what to say or do in order to maintain the truth *and* good relationships.

Be Tender

*"Blessed are the meek, for they
will inherit the earth."*
Matthew 5:5

Let's be gentle and sensitive when we are touching the tender feelings of others. Moms and dads, it's hard to exaggerate the value of tact within the walls of your home. Soften the blows a little! You'll preserve some very valuable self-esteem while gaining much-needed respect.

JULY 25

COME ASIDE AND LEARN
ABOUT BEING TACTFUL

*Therefore, although in Christ I
could be bold and order you to
do what you ought to do, yet I
appeal to you on the basis of love ...*
Philemon 8-9

Paul's brief letter to Philemon – regarding
the return of a runaway slave – is a model
of tact and wisdom in a potentially divisive situation. Read through it and mentally give Paul a compliment each time he
shows good judgment in his choice of
words.

WHEN PRAISE ERUPTS

*I praise you because I am fearfully and
wonderfully made; your works are
wonderful, I know that full well.*
Psalm 139:14

Words from one of my mentors: "Wonder
is involuntary praise."

GOD'S CREATION IS VAST

*"... Surely I spoke of things I
did not understand, things too
wonderful for me to know."*
Job 42:3

If it were possible to travel the speed of light, you could arrive at the moon in one-and-a-third seconds. But continuing that same speed, do you know how long it would take you to reach the closest star? Four years. Incredible thought! The boggled mind leads to a bended knee.

The Language Of Creation

For the truth about God is known to them instinctively; God has put this knowledge in their hearts. Since earliest times men have seen the earth and sky and all God made, and have known of his existence and great eternal power. So they will have no excuse (when they stand before God at Judgment Day).
Romans 1:19-20 (TLB)

TAKE TIME TO READ!

But his delight is in the law of the Lord, and on his law he meditates day and night ... Whatever he does prospers.
Psalm 1:2-3

Here are some benefits of reading: Reading sweeps the cobwebs away. Reading increases our power of concentration. Reading makes us more interesting to be around. Reading strengthens our ability to glean truth from God's Word.

JUST A LITTLE BIT MORE!

"... If anyone wants to be first, he must be the very last, and the servant of all."
Mark 9:35

The wealthy John D. Rockefeller was once asked, "How much does it take to satisfy a man?" With rare wisdom he answered, "A little bit more than he has."

CONTENTMENT

*"For where your treasure is,
there your heart will be also."*
Luke 12:34

Does contentment mean I need to sell all my possessions and never buy anything new? Does it mean I cannot have nice things? No – it just means those nice things don't possess you.

AUGUST

The Shores Of Lake Contentment

Do not be anxious about anything, but in everything, by prayer and petition, with thanksgiving, present your requests to God.
Philippians 4:6

What a beautiful scene in the soul is Lake Contentment! Undisturbed by outside noises brought on by the jackhammers of exaggeration, those who enjoy the lake know what relaxation is all about. They know nothing of any winter of discontent – or spring or fall or summer, for that matter. Such an existence breeds security and happiness.

Come Aside And Grow In Contentment

*When you send your Spirit, they
are created ... May the glory
of the Lord endure forever ...*
Psalm 104:30-31

Escape from the prison walls of reinforced materialism, and breathe the Lord's free air in Psalm 104. Slowly. Please.

Silence

Even a fool is thought wise if
he keeps silent, and discerning
if he holds his tongue.
Proverbs 17:28

The way to show yourself wise is not so much by speech but by silence.

POSITIVE MODELS

A gentle answer turns away wrath,
but a harsh word stirs up anger.
Proverbs 15:1

The way to stop a loud argument is by a soft-spoken word. The most powerful rebuke is not a loud, negative blast, but a quiet, positive model.

TRUST

*He is my refuge and my fortress,
my God, in whom I trust.*
Psalm 91:2

The secret of helping others mature is not more rules and stricter laws but greater trust.

GENEROUS GIVERS

"Give to the one who asks you,
and do not turn away from the one
who wants to borrow from you."
Matthew 5:42

Those who give generously have much more than those who hoard.

Handling Our Enemies

... live at peace with everyone.
Do not take revenge, my friends,
but leave room for God's wrath ...
Romans 12:18-19

Forgiveness is the key to handling our enemies, not revenge.

Overcome Evil
With Good

Do not be overcome by evil,
but overcome evil with good.
Romans 12:21

The most effective form of retaliation is an *absence* of retaliation ... leaving all vengeance to God. In doing so, to quote the Scriptures, we "heap burning coals upon the head" of an adversary, which is nothing more than overcoming evil with good.

Sympathy

*A man of knowledge uses
words with restraint ...*
Proverbs 17:27

A brief, warm, tender embrace with very
few words says more to the grieving than
an evening's visit full of sympathy talk,
Scripture quoting, and long prayers.

COME ASIDE AND REFLECT ON THE WAYS OF GOD

Who, being in the very nature
God ... made himself nothing,
taking the very nature of a servant,
being made in human likeness ...
Philippians 2:6-7

Be in awe of the ways of God as you read again in Philippians 2:5-11 about the greatest contradiction in eternal history.

When There Is No Healing

That is why, for Christ's sake, I delight in weaknesses, in insults, in hardships, in persecutions, in difficulties. For when I am weak, then I am strong.
2 Corinthians 12:10

Three times Paul asked God to remove the thorn. Three times he got a "no" answer (*2 Corinthians 12:7-9*). Following that traumatic experience he stated he was "well content with weaknesses ... difficulties" (*2 Corinthians 12:10*) because even without healing, the Lord proved Himself sufficient and strong in the apostle's life.

AUGUST 12

WHEN THERE IS HEALING

*Who forgives all your sins
and heals all your diseases.*
Psalm 103:3

Every time healing happens, God has done it. It occurs daily. Occasionally it is miraculous. More often, it is aided by proper diagnosis, competent medical care, essential medicinal assistance, plus common sense. No hocus pocus. No mumbo jumbo. But whenever God heals there is *no way* any person can grab the glory.

Hit The Brakes ...
While You Still Can

There is a time for everything, and a season for every activity under heaven.
Ecclesiastes 3:1

If you are involved in church or religious activities to the point that your home life is hurting, you're too involved – and you're heading for trouble. The law of diminishing returns will soon catch up with you.

THE HOME

Unless the Lord builds the house,
its builders labor in vain ...
Psalm 127:1

The church can seldom resurrect what the home puts to death. The very best proof of the genuineness of your Christianity occurs within the framework of your home. If you must become overinvolved – become overinvolved in your role as a character builder in the home.

Cultivate The
Soul With Care

And because the midwives feared God,
he gave them families of their own.
Exodus 1:21

The church will stay healthy and strong as long as its homes are healthy and strong. God's priority system seems to begin at the grassroots level – at home.

COME ASIDE AND GROW IN YOUR FAMILY LIFE

*Submit to one another out
of reverence for Christ.*
Ephesians 5:21

*Fathers, do not exasperate your
children; instead, bring them up in the
training and instruction of the Lord.*
Ephesians 6:4

Review Ephesians 5:21 through 6:4, and ask God to show you *one* way in which you can better obey one of these commands before this day is over.

CATCH IT!

Brothers, I do not consider myself yet to have taken hold of it. But one thing I do: Forgetting what is behind and straining toward what is ahead, I press on toward the goal to win the prize for which God has called me heavenward in Christ Jesus.
Philippians 3:13-14

Vision is contagious!

YOU ARE INVITED

Come to Me, all who are weary and heavy laden, and I will give you rest. Take My yoke upon you, and learn from Me, for I am gentle and humble in heart; and you shall find rest for your souls. For My yoke is easy, and My load is light.
Matthew 11:28-30 (NASB)

What restful words: easy ... light.

REST

The Lord gave them rest on every side, just as he had sworn to their forefathers ...
Joshua 21:44

While so many are demanding, Jesus is gentle. While competition is rugged and being in partnership with hard-charging, bullish leaders is tough, being yoked with Him is easy. Yes, *easy*. And instead of increasing our load of anxiety, He promises to make it lighter.

Quiet Shores

*The Lord is my shepherd, I shall not be
in want. He makes me lie down in green
pastures, he leads me beside quiet waters.*
Psalm 23:1-2

Where do you go to find enough stillness
to rediscover that God is God? Where do
you turn when your days and nights start
running together? As in days of old, Jesus
is waiting in that little boat, ready to sail
with you to a quieter shore. But *getting* in
first requires letting go.

Come Aside And Trust

"And if I go and prepare a place for you, I will come back and take you to be with me that you also may be where I am."
John 14:3

Let it be just you and the Lord, and let your mind be only on Him, as you hear each word of love for you in John 14:1-4.

DO YOUR PART!

*Noah did everything just
as God commanded him.*
Genesis 6:22

Hope for our great nation rests upon independent thinking and individual effort. The revival of discipline, integrity, work, determination, and healthy pride is not a national matter but a *personal* one. Inward change and godliness are not legislated by congress — they are spawned in the heart and cultivated in the home before they are bred in the land. Frankly, it boils down to one person, *you*.

A Picture Of Discontentment

Delight yourself in the Lord and he will give you the desires of your heart.
Psalm 37:4

The plague of pursuit: pushing, straining, stretching, relentlessly reaching while our minds become strangled with the lie, "enough isn't enough." What a consuming passion ... yet how empty, how unsatisfying!

Perspective

Commit your way to the Lord;
trust in him and he will do this.
Psalm 37:5

One who views life through perspective lenses has the capacity to see things in their true relations or relative importance. He sees the big picture. He is able to distinguish the essential from the incidental ... the forest from the trees.

WHERE TO FIND PERSPECTIVE

*Find rest, O my soul, in God
alone; my hope comes from him.*
Psalm 62:5

Many things help prompt perspective. Quietness. A walk in a forest. A stroll along a crashing surf. A view from a mountain. Poetry. Deep, profound strains of music. Protracted time of prayer. Meaningful worship. Meditation upon Scripture. A leisurely drive at sunset. Go ahead ... take time.

COME ASIDE AND FIND PERSPECTIVE

Consider him who endured such opposition from sinful men, so that you will not grow weary and lose heart.
Hebrews 12:3

Stand aside from the rush of life and meditate for a while on Hebrews 12:1-3.

Jesus Lifts Us

*Now if we died with Christ, we believe
that we will also live with him.*
Romans 6:8

Life, with all its pressures and inequities,
tears and tragedies, can be lived on a level
above its miseries.

In The Pressure Cooker

When he has stood the test, he will receive the crown of life that God has promised to those who love him.
James 1:12

It is upon the platform of pressure that our Lord does His best work ... those times when tragedy joins hands with calamity. At such times Christ unsheathes His sword of truth, silencing the doubts and offering grace to accept, hope to continue.

WHEN SORROW VISITS

*"... you will weep and mourn while
the world rejoices. You will grieve,
but your grief will turn to joy."*
John 16:20

Sorrow and her grim family of sighs may drop by for a visit, but they won't stay long when they realize faith got there first ... and doesn't plan to leave.

LOOK IN THE MIRROR

Get rid of the old yeast that
you may be a new batch without
yeast – as you really are ...
1 Corinthians 5:7

It .is essential that we see ourselves as we really are in the light of God's written Word ... then be open to change where change is needed. I warn you, the number one enemy of change is the hard-core, self-satisfied sin nature within you. Change is among its *greatest* threats.

WE ARE GOD'S PERSONAL PROJECTS

So God created man in his own image,
in the image of God he created him;
male and female he created them.
Genesis 1:27

God is committed to the task of working in us, developing us, rearranging, firming up, and deepening us so that the character traits of His Son begin to take shape. The emerging of the Son's image in us is of primary importance to the Father.

SEPTEMBER

A Persian Proverb

For the Lord gives wisdom,
and from his mouth come
knowledge and understanding.
Proverbs 2:6

He who knows not, and knows not that he knows not, is a fool; shun him. He who knows not, and knows that he knows not is a child; teach him. He who knows, and knows not that he knows, is asleep; wake him. He who knows, and knows that he knows is wise; follow him.

SOLOMON SEEKS DISCERNMENT

*When God told Solomon to make a wish —
any wish — and it would be granted, the
king responded: "Give Thy servant an
understanding heart to judge Thy people
and to discern between good and evil."*
1 Kings 3:9 (NASB)

Solomon desired the ability to detect and
identify real truth. To see beneath the
surface and correctly be able to "size up" a
situation. To read between the lines of the
visible. May we be like Solomon and see
the importance of discernment and seek
after it.

THINK WITH DISCERNMENT

How many are your works, O Lord!
In wisdom you made them all; the
earth is full of your creatures.
Psalm 104:24

Discernment gives one a proper frame of reference, a definite line separating good and evil. It acts as an umpire in life and blows the whistle on the spurious. It's as particular as a pathologist peering into a microscope. Discernment picks and chooses its dates with great care. It doesn't fall for fakes ... or flirt with phonies ... or dance with deceivers ... or kiss counterfeits goodnight.

DISCERNING THE SLEEPING FROM THE WISE

*Understanding is a fountain
of life to those who have it, but
folly brings punishment to fools.*
Proverbs 16:22

Discernment would rather relax alone at night with the Good Book than mess around with the gullible gang. You see, it's from that Book that discernment learns to distinguish the fools from the children ... and the sleeping from the wise.

WHERE TO GO TO FIND DISCERNMENT

If any of you lacks wisdom, he should ask God, who gives generously to all without finding fault, and it will be given to him. But when he asks, he must believe and not doubt, because he who doubts is like a wave of the sea, blown and tossed by the wind.
James 1:5-6

Go to your *knees*. God's Word promises wisdom to those who ask for it.

WHERE TO GO TO FIND DISCERNMENT

Your commands make me wiser than my enemies, for they are ever with me. I have more understanding than the elders, for I obey your precepts.
Psalm 119:98, 100

Go to the Word. Read Psalm 119:98-100. You will find insight beyond your fondest dreams.

WHERE TO GO TO FIND DISCERNMENT

*Go to the ant, you sluggard;
consider its ways and be wise!*
Proverbs 6:6

Go to the *wise*. Discernment is better caught than taught.

COME ASIDE AND SET PRIORITIES

For this very reason, make every effort to add to your faith goodness; and to goodness, knowledge; and to knowledge, self-control; and to self-control, perseverance and to perseverance, godliness; and to godliness, brotherly kindness, and to brotherly kindness, love. For if you possess these qualities in increasing measure, they will keep you from being ineffective and unproductive in your knowledge of our Lord Jesus Christ.
2 Peter 1:5-8

Make a priority list of the most important tasks you want to accomplish in the next twenty-four hours.

Purposeful Living

*Look carefully then how you walk! Live
purposefully and worthily and accurately, not
as the unwise and witless, but as wise (sensible,
intelligent people). Making the very most of the
time (buying up each opportunity), because the
days are evil. Therefore do not be vague and
thoughtless and foolish, but understanding and
firmly grasping what the will of the Lord is.*
Ephesians 5:15-17 (AMP)

It's About Time

Making the most of every opportunity ...
Ephesians 5:16

The easiest thing in the world is to drift through life in a vague, thoughtless manner. God says there's a better way. He tells us to take time by the throat, give it a good shake, and declare: "That's it! I'm going to manage you – no longer will you manage me!"

Living Above Our Circumstances

My times are in your hands ...
Psalm 31:15

Remember these things as you seek to manage your time: Be punctual. Start early. Pace yourself. Finish strong.

SQUEAKY WHEELS

... for there will be a time for every activity, a time for every deed.
Ecclesiastes 3:17

Time management allows room for ease and humor, much-needed oil to soothe the friction created by motion.

Megachanges

*"I the Lord do not change. So you, O
descendants of Jacob, are not destroyed."*
Malachi 3:6

Extraordinary times will require of us extraordinary wisdom, vision, boldness, flexibility, dedication, willingness to adapt, and a renewed commitment to biblical principles that never change. The secret, of course, is adapting to our times without altering God's truth.

COME ASIDE AND HEAR WHAT GOD HAS TO SAY TO YOU

"Who then is able to stand against me? Who has a claim against me that I must pay? Everything under heaven belongs to me."
Job 41:10-11

Beginning in Job 38:1, read as much as you have time for of this stormy message from the Lord to Job (it continues through chapter 41). What is God communicating here to you?

After The Avalanche

*... In all this, Job did not
sin in what he said.*
Job 2:10

Job could write about wounds. He lost
his livestock, crops, land, servants, and –
if you can believe it – all ten children. Soon
thereafter he lost his health. How could
anyone handle such a series of grief-laden
ordeals so calmly? Think of the aftermath:
bankruptcy, pain, ten fresh graves. Yet we
read in Job that he worshiped God; he did
not sin, nor did he blame his Maker.

JOB LOOKED UP

"... Shall we accept good from
God, and not trouble?..."
Job 2:10

Job claimed God's loving sovereignty. He sincerely believed that the Lord who gave had every right to remove. Who is the fool that says God has no right to add sand to our clay or marks to our vessel or fire to His workmanship? Not Job! To him, God's sovereignty was laced with His love.

JOB LOOKED AHEAD

And hope does not disappoint us, because God has poured out his love into our hearts by the Holy Spirit, whom he has given us.
Romans 5:5

Job counted on the promise of resurrection. He counted on his Lord's promise to make all things bright and beautiful in the life beyond. He knew that at *that* time, all pain, death, sorrow, tears, and adversity would be removed. Knowing that "... hope does not disappoint ..." (*Romans 5:5*), he endured today by envisioning tomorrow.

JOB LOOKED WITHIN

*"'Who is this that obscures my counsel
without knowledge?' Surely I spoke of
things I did not understand ..."*
Job 42:3

Job confessed his own lack of understanding. What a relief this brings! Job didn't feel obligated to explain the "whys" of his situation. He confessed his inability to put it all together. Resting his case with the righteous Judge, Job did not feel compelled to answer all the questions or unravel all the burning riddles. God would judge. The Judge would be right.

A Little Rain
Helps Us Grow

*I planted the seed, Apollos watered
it, but God made it grow.*
1 Corinthians 3:6

Cloudless days are fine, but remember:
Some pottery gets pretty fragile sitting in
the sun day after day after day.

WARNING!

*"But I tell you that anyone who looks at
a woman lustfully has already committed
adultery with her in his heart."*
Matthew 5:28

Lust is one flame you dare not fan. You'll
get burned if you do.

COME ASIDE AND LEARN HOW TO CLOSE THE DOOR TO LUST

*That each of you should learn
to control his own body in a way
that is holy and honorable, not in
passionate lust ... and that in this matter
no one should wrong his brother ...*
1 Thessalonians 4:4-6

Search through 1 Thessalonians 4:1-2 and find at least three guidelines for how to close your door to lust. Write them down on a card and keep it available.

Closing The Door To Lust

Put on the full armor of God so
that you can take your stand
against the devil's schemes.
Ephesians 6:11

Lust is no respecter of persons. No one is immune. You're not. I'm not. And beware – it never gives up ... it never runs out of ideas. How do you handle such an aggressive intruder? Try this: When lust suggests a rendezvous, send Jesus Christ as your representative.

SOMETHING BETTER

For he himself is our peace ...
Ephesians 2:14

Before giving lust a firm shove away from your life, have Christ inform this intruder that the permanent peace and pleasure you are enjoying in your new home with Christ are so much greater than lust's temporary excitement that you don't need it around any longer to keep you happy.

SUPERSTITION

*"So if the Son sets you free,
you will be free indeed."*
John 8:36

The goal of superstition is *bondage*. If *anything* in your Christianity has you in bondage, it is probable that some form of superstition is the breeding ground. You see, our Savior came to give us the truth and set us free. Superstition, although prompted by sincerity, brings the plague of slavery. Sincerity doesn't liberate; Christ does.

Who Cares?

*Do not forget to entertain strangers,
for by so doing some people have
entertained angels without knowing it.*
Hebrews 13:2

Deep within many a forgotten life is a scrap of hope, a lonely melody trying hard to return. Some are in prison. Some in hospitals. Some in nursing homes. And some silently slip into church on Sunday morning, terribly confused and afraid. Do you care? Enough "to show hospitality to strangers," as Hebrews 13:2 (NASB) puts it?

Come Aside And Reflect On Jesus' Compassion

"What do you think? If a man owns a hundred sheep, and one of them wanders away, will he not leave the ninety-nine on the hills and go to look for the one that wandered off? And if he finds it, I tell you the truth, he is happier about one sheep than the ninety-nine that did not wander off.
Matthew 18:12-13

WHAT TO DO DURING THE OFFERING?

... and the wise heart will know the proper time and procedure. For there is a proper time and procedure for every matter ...
Ecclesiastes 8:5-6

Here are the few practical suggestions on what to do to make the most of the time during the offering: 1. Take a pencil along with the bulletin stub and write down a list of the things for which you are most grateful. 2. Turn to the Scripture that will be used in the sermon. Read it over slowly. 3. Pray for someone sitting near you. 4. Pray for the one who will bring the message.

A Bond That Binds

Love is patient, love is kind ... it is not self-seeking ... It always protects, always trusts, always hopes, always perseveres.
1 Corinthians 13:4-5, 7

There is a bond deep within that binds us to one another. It is the glue of authentic love, expressing itself in compassion, fairness, willingness to support, and (when possible) coming to the aid of another. Personally. Without strings attached. Committed to the protection and dignity of human life.

BIGNESS

*This is how we know what love is:
Jesus Christ laid down his life for
us. And we ought to lay down
our lives for our brothers.*
1 John 3:16

What is bigness? Being free of grudges, pettiness, envy, vengeance, and prejudice. Seeing another in need – regardless of differences of opinion – and reaching out in solid Christian maturity. Just because you care.

Bigness Is Rare

Be devoted to one another in brotherly love. Honor one another above yourselves.
Romans 12:10

Bigness is living above labels ... it's seeing beyond hurts ... it's caring unconditionally, helping unassumingly. And therefore it's rare. As rare as a hawk and a dove in the same nest on a cold winter's night.

OCTOBER

What Is Your Testimony?

*Many of the Samaritans from
that town believed in him
because of the woman's testimony ...*
John 4:39

One time-honored and effective method of evangelism is the giving of your personal testimony. The skeptic may deny your doctrine or attack your church but he cannot honestly ignore the fact that your life has been changed. If you have not discovered the value of telling others how God rearranged and transformed your life, you've missed a vital link in the chain of His blessing.

Your Testimony: Be Interesting

My mouth will speak words of wisdom; the utterance from my heart will give understanding.
Psalm 49:3

No one, no matter how gracious, enjoys being bored. It's a contradiction to talk about how exciting Christ really is in an uninteresting way. Work on your wording, your flow of thought, your key terms. Remember, the person you are talking to isn't saved so guard against religious clichés and hard-to-understand terminology. Keep it interesting!

YOUR TESTIMONY: BE LOGICAL

When they had testified and proclaimed the word of the Lord ...
Acts 8:25

Think of your salvation in three phases ... and construct your testimony accordingly: (a) before you were born again – the loneliness, lack of peace, absence of love, unrest and fears; (b) the decision that revolutionized your life; and (c) the change, the difference He has made since you received Christ.

YOUR TESTIMONY: BE SPECIFIC

For in the gospel a righteousness from God is revealed, a righteousness that is by faith from first to last ...
Romans 1:17

Be extremely careful here as you tell your story, because you want the moment of your new birth to be clear. Don't be at all vague regarding how you became a Christian. Speak of Christ, not the church. Refer to the decision you made, the moment of time when you received the Lord. Spell out the specifics. Be simple and direct. Emphasize faith more than feeling.

Your Testimony: Be Practical

In everything set them an example by doing what is good. In your teaching show integrity, seriousness and soundness of speech that cannot be condemned ...
Titus 2:7-8

Be human and honest as you talk. Don't promise, "All your problems will end if you will become a Christian," for that isn't true. Try to think as an unbeliever thinks while speaking. Refuse to pick theological lint. Restrain yourself from plucking wings off religious flies. Theoretical stuff doesn't attract the other person's attention as much as practical reality.

YOUR TESTIMONY: BE WARM AND GENUINE

Now this is our boast: Our consciene testifies that we have conducted ourselves ... in the holiness and sincerity that are from God ...
2 Corinthians 1:12

A smile breaks down more barriers than the hammer blows of cold, hard facts. Be friendly and sincere. Let your enthusiasm flow freely. It's hard to convince another person of the sheer joy and excitement of knowing Christ if you're wearing a jail-warden face. Above all, be positive and courteous. (One final bit of advice: be sure you don't have bad breath!)

COME ASIDE: AN ENCOUNTER WITH JESUS

... he was met by a demon-possessed man from the town. For a long time this man had not worn clothes or lived in a house, but had lived in the tombs. The man from whom the demons had gone out begged to go with him (Jesus) ...
Luke 8:27, 38

Review the amazing account of one man's encounter with Jesus in Luke 8:26-39. Try to sense how this man must have felt after the Lord freed him.

STAY IN CIRCULATION

To this you were called, because Christ suffered for you, leaving you an example, that you should follow in his steps.
1 Peter 2:21

The practical goal of authentic Christianity is not rows of silver saints, highly polished, frequently dusted, crammed into the corners of elegant cathedrals ... Not plaster people cloaked in thin layers of untarnished silver and topped with a metallic halo ... But *real* people. Melted saints circulating through the mainstream of humanity, bringing worth and value down where life transpires in the raw.

What An Honor!

*Consequently, you are no longer foreigners
and aliens, but fellow citizens with God's
people and members of God's household.*
Ephesians 2:19

Being among the saints is no sacrifice ...
it's a brief, choice privilege.

DOING BATTLE IN THE JUNGLE

For our struggle is not against flesh and blood, but against the rulers, against the authorities, against the powers of this dark world and against the spiritual forces of evil in the heavenly realms.
Ephesians 6:12

No rhinestone cowboys can cut it among the swamps and insects of the gross world system. Sunday-go-to-meetin' silver saints in shining armor are simply out of circulation if that's the limit to their faith. Waging wilderness warfare calls for sweat ... energy ... keen strategy ... determination ... a good supply of ammunition ... willingness to fight ... refusal to surrender. Most of all, a positive, enthusiastic attitude.

WHY WE MUST BE MELTED

"Make every effort to enter through the narrow door ..."
Luke 13:24

Those who successfully wage war with silent heroism under relentless secular pressure – ah, *they* are the saints who know what it means to be melted. It's all part of remaining "in circulation."

INFIDELITY DISPLEASES GOD

*Let marriage be held in honor among all,
and let the marriage bed be undefiled; for
fornicators and adulterers God will judge.*
Hebrews 13:4 (NASB)

Finding intimacy outside your marriage
with someone other than your mate *isn't*
okay. It's sinful. It doesn't simplify life, it
complicates. It won't satisfy, it will bring
ruin.

COME ASIDE AND ALLOW GOD TO MEET YOUR NEEDS

I spread out my hands to you; my soul thirsts for you like a parched land.
Psalm 143:6

Deceiving yourself isn't healthy, it's sick. It doesn't prove you're independent and strong ... it's a declaration that you've got deep needs. Read Psalm 143 to help you enter God's presence and present those needs to Him.

THE DESTRUCTION OF INFIDELITY

The righteousness of the upright delivers them, but the unfaithful are trapped by evil desires.
Proverbs 11:6

Infidelity causes pain to others. Infidelity masks the real problem. Infidelity is destructive to self.

Artificial Turf

*"... anyone who looks at a woman
lustfully has already committed
adultery with her in his heart."*
Matthew 5:27

The grass of an illicit affair may indeed
look greener on the other side of the fence.
But it's poison. A loving God put the fence
there for a reason.

A Touch Of Class

You will be made rich in every way so that you can be generous on every occasion ...
2 Corinthians 9:11

God's Word encourages us to be prudent individuals, but generous (dare I say *extravagant*?) with Him. Time and again in the pages of God's Book saints are exhorted to be magnanimous, liberal, openhanded ... to such an extreme that some today would find themselves almost ill at ease surrounded by such opulent loveliness.

Humility And Beauty

*King Solomon was greater in
riches and wisdom than all
the other kings of the earth.*
1 Kings 10:23

Why have we embraced the idea that elegance and class have no place on the spectrum of spirituality? What makes us less comfortable working and worshiping in lovely surroundings than in plain ones? Who ever said that humility and beauty cannot co-exist?

Make It Clear!

*The word is near you; it is in
your mouth and in your heart, that
is, the word of faith we are proclaiming.*
Romans 10:8

When we express our faith, we must be careful not to toss around terms familiar only to the "in" group, in phrases foreign to those in the world system (and then blame *them* for not being interested!). Our secret language calls for a decoding process non-Christians aren't equipped to handle. How much better to talk in a plain, concrete, believable manner so the Spirit of God has the ammunition needed to complete the task.

THE INFALLIBLILITY OF SCRIPTURE

"... your word is truth."
John 17:17

The infallibility of Scripture is a watershed issue. Take away that absolute and you've opened an unpluggable hole in your theological dike. Given enough time and pressure, it wouldn't be long before everything around you would get soggy and slippery.

COME ASIDE AND THANK GOD

Your word, O Lord, is eternal; it stands firm in the heavens. Your faithfulness continues through all generations ...
Psalm 119:89-90

Thank God for the infallibility of His Word as you review Psalm 119:89-96.

INFALLIBILITY AND FALLIBILITY

There is not a righteous man on earth who does what is right and never sins.
Ecclesiastes 7:20

Just as biblical infallibility assures us that each page is incapable of error or deception, fallibility reminds us that each person is capable of both. The implications are equally clear. When it comes to the Bible, keep trusting. When it comes to people, be discerning.

THE SOURCE OF GROWTH

It is God who arms me with strength ...
Psalm 18:32

So then neither the one who plants nor the one who waters is anything, but God who causes the growth.
1 Corinthians 3:7 (NASB)

Healthy Skepticism

Do not put your trust in princes,
in mortal men, who cannot save.
Psalm 146:3

All men are created fallible. Yes, all. If you remember that, you'll have fewer surprises and disappointments, greater wisdom, and a whole lot better perspective in life.

THE END OF THE ROAD

For the word of God is living and active ...
Hebrews 4:12

If you're looking for infallibility, look no further than God's Word. His messengers are not; His message is.

Someone's Watching You!

*But just as he who called you is
holy, so be holy in all you do.*
1 Peter 1:15

Growing young Christians are watching you! How much stability, integrity, courtesy, and decisiveness are you demonstrating?

THE SMALL STUFF

*Jesus said, "Let the little children
come to me, and do not hinder
them, for the kingdom of
heaven belongs to such as these."*
Matthew 19:14

Greatness and the attention to detail are
welded together.

Come Aside And Do Something Special

So whether you eat or drink or whatever you do, do it all for the glory of God.
1 Corinthians 10:31

Decide now to do something special in the next twenty-four hours – something no one may ever notice except you and your Creator – in which you can demonstrate high-quality workmanship.

HANDLING OUR CONFLICTS

And the Lord's servant must not quarrel; instead, he must be kind to everyone, able to teach, not resentful.
2 Timothy 2:24

The spirit with which we handle our conflicts and the attitudes we exhibit while working through the process of reconciliation is crucial ... *that* is where our Christianity is often hung out to dry.

THE DANGER OF PRIDE

*... God opposes the proud
but gives grace to the humble.*
James 4:6

When the head swells, the heart hardens.

FOLLOW GOD'S EXAMPLE

*Get rid of all bitterness, rage and anger,
brawling and slander, along with every
form of malice. Be kind and compassionate
to one another, forgiving each other, just
as in Christ God forgave you.*
Ephesians 4:31-32 (PHILLIPS)

Let there be no more bitter resentment or anger, no more shouting or slander, and let there be no bad feeling of any kind among you. Be kind to each other, be compassionate. Be as ready to forgive others as God for Christ's sake has forgiven you.

The Joy Of Gratitude

... And be thankful.
Colossians 3:15

What brings about the joy of gratitude? It's receiving what we *don't* deserve. When that happens, humility replaces pride. A thankful spirit cancels out arrogance. A conceited spirit and a humble heart don't occupy the same body.

NOVEMBER

REMEMBERING NAMES

*"The virgin will be with child and will give
birth to a son, and they will call him
Immanuel – which means, 'God with us.'"*
Matthew 1:23

You *can* remember names! The secret lies
in that very brief period of time we stand
face to face with another person. You see,
that momentary encounter has been di-
rected by God. He has arranged two lives
so that they cross at His prescribed time –
so you can be sure that the meeting is
significant. So is the name! Zero in first on
one major thing – *the name*. Listen for one
thing, *the name*.

A Name Is Important!

"... To him who overcomes, I will give some of the hidden manna. I will also give him a white stone with a new name written on it, known only to him who receives it."
Revelation 2:17

If the Lord thinks enough of our names to write every one of them in His record, is it asking too much to learn a few as we travel here below? Of course this means that we must consider the other person important enough to remember. If you struggle with *that* you have a problem far more serious than a faulty memory!

IF ONLY

Reckless words pierce like a sword, but the tongue of the wise brings healing.
Proverbs 12:18

Think before you speak. Pause before you act.

COME ASIDE AND SET PRIORITIES

Above all, love each other deeply ...
so that in all things God may be
praised through Jesus Christ ...
1 Peter 4:8, 11

Fix your thoughts for a while on the handful of priorities presented in 1 Peter 4:7-11. Read slowly. How well are you doing?

Getting It Right The First Time

The king talked with them, and
he found none equal to Daniel ...
And Daniel remained there
until the first year of King Cyrus.
Daniel 1:19, 21

We never have a second chance to make a first impression. Initial impressions cannot be remade. Cutting remarks cannot be re-said. Scars can't be completely removed. Tear stains on the delicate fabric of our emotions are, more often than not, permanent. Memories are fixed, not flexible. Today is memory in the making, a deposit in the bank of time. Let's make each one a good one!

Is It Urgent Or Important?

Turn my eyes away from worthless things;
preserve my life according to your word.
Psalm 119:37

In the now-or-later battle for priorities, it's clear where the secret lies. Let's take care of the biggies now — today. It's amazing how the incidentals will fade away when we focus fully on the essentials. And that's impossible unless we put the important ahead of the urgent.

BUILDING THE
FUTURE TODAY

... Today, if you hear his voice.
Psalm 95:7

What will be yesterday's replays in the tomorrows of your life? The answer is not that complicated. They will be the things your "walls" are absorbing today.

PROSPERITY PUT TO THE TEST

"... I tell you the truth, it is hard for a rich man to enter the kingdom of heaven."
Matthew 19:23

Precious few are those who can live in the lap of luxury ... who can keep their moral, spiritual, and financial equilibrium. It's ironic that most of us can handle a sudden demotion much better than a sizable promotion. Here's why. When adversity strikes, life becomes rather simple. Our need is reduced to *survival*. But when prosperity occurs, life gets complicated. Our needs become numerous and often extremely complex. Invariably, our integrity is put to the test.

Dancing With Success

"It is easier for a camel to go through the eye of a needle than for a rich man to enter the kingdom of God."
Mark 10:25

There is about one in a hundred who can dance to the tune of success without paying the piper named Compromise.

INTEGRITY UNVEILED

When you make a vow to God, do not delay in fulfilling it ... fulfill your vow.
Ecclesiastes 5:4

When you give your word, you do it. Exactly as you said you would. Because integrity means you are verbally trustworthy. When bills come due, you pay them. Because integrity means you are financially dependable. When you're tempted to mess around with an illicit sexual affair, you resist. Because integrity means you are morally pure.

COME ASIDE AND REFLECT ON YOUR LIFE

"He gave you manna to eat in the desert,
something your fathers had never known,
to humble and to test you so that in the end
it might go well with you. You may say to
yourself, 'My power and the strength of my
hands have produced this wealth for me.'"
Deuteronomy 8:16-17

Read Deuteronomy 8 to uncover rich lessons about dealing with both adversity and prosperity. Then, considering how life is going for you these days, decide which important truth in this passage you need most to remember.

BALANCE

*"... Shall we accept good from
God, and not trouble? ..."*
Job 2:10

Adversity or prosperity, both are tough tests
on our balance. To stay balanced through
prosperity – ah, that demands *integrity*. The
swift wind of compromise is a lot more
devastating than the sudden jolt of misfor-
tune. That's why walking on a wire is
harder than standing up in a storm. Height
has a strange way of disturbing our balance.

So Many Have It;
So Few Use It!

For the word of God is living and active.
Sharper than any double-edged sword,
it penetrates even to dividing soul and
spirit, joints and marrow; it judges the
thoughts and attitudes of the heart.
Hebrews 4:12

We have the Scriptures in hardback, paperback, cloth, and leather ... versions and paraphrases too numerous to count ... redletter editions along with various sizes of print on the page ... Bibles as big as a library dictionary and small as one frame of microfilm ... yet the years roll by as one generation after another passes on its biblical illiteracy.

STOP IGNORANCE

But, dear friends, remember what the apostles of our Lord Jesus Christ foretold.
Jude verse 17

Biblical ignorance is a personal choice – *your choice*. If something is going to plug the dike, it will take *your* finger to stop the leak.

Beware Of Idols

*Little children, guard
yourselves from idols.*
1 John 5:21 (NASB)

This was the apostle John's final warning to his readers. "Watch out," says John. "Be on guard against anything that might occupy the place in your heart that should be reserved for the Living God."

Put Jesus First

"You shall not make for yourself an idol in the form of anything … You shall not bow down to them or worship them; for I, the Lord your God, am a jealous God …"
Deuteronomy 5:8-9

Any idol, regardless of its beauty or usefulness or original purpose, is to be set aside so that Christ might reign supreme, without a single rival.

IDENTIFYING IDOLS

"Anyone who loves his father or mother more than me is not worthy of me; anyone who loves his son or daughter more than me is not worthy of me."
Matthew 10:37

You can make an idol out of anything or anyone in life. A church building can become an idol to us. Your mate or child can be given first place in your life and literally idolized. Your work, house, car, education, or even the goal of "retirement" can become your god. There's nothing necessarily wrong with any of these good things. To possess them is not sinful. But it is sinful when they *possess us!*

First Place
In Everything

*For by him all things were created
... He is before all things, and
in him all things hold together.*
Colossians 1:16-17

He is also head of the body, the church;
and He is the beginning, the first-born from
the dead; so that He Himself might come
to have first place in everything.
Colossians 1:18 (NASB)

COME ASIDE AND REMOVE THE IDOLS IN YOUR LIFE

"... Get rid of the foreign gods you have with you ... Then come, let us go up to Bethel, where I will build an altar to God, who answered me ..."
Genesis 35:2-3

Waste no time in asking God to help you realize and remove any idols that are usurping His place in your heart. Use Genesis 35:1-4 as an example to guide you through the cleansing process. Then spend time in worship, meditating on Psalm 29.

NOVEMBER 20

Running Shy Of Eagles

Preach the Word; be prepared in season and out of season ...
2 Timothy 4:2

Content to sit safely on our evangelical perches and repeat in rapid-fire falsetto our religious words, we are fast becoming overpopulated with bright-colored birds having soft bellies, big beaks, and little heads. What would help to balance things out would be a lot more keen-eyed, wide-winged creatures willing to soar out and up, exploring the illimitable ranges of the kingdom of God. We could use a lot more eagles and no more parrots!

Unwanted People

Do not repay anyone evil for evil. Be careful to do what is right in the eyes of everybody.
Romans 12:17

Instead of loving difficult people, we usually label them. Instead of caring, we criticize. Instead of getting next to them, we react, we resent, we run. Instead of "kissing the frog," we develop ways of poisoning it – or at best, ignoring it completely. None of this is easy ... but it is Christlike.

BUILDING BRIDGES TO THE OUTCAST

Each of you should look not only to your own interests, but also to the interests of others.
Philippians 2:4

Be positive rather than negative. Ask yourself, "Lord, how can I express Your love?"
Be gracious rather than irritated. Respond in grace and kindness and it will often unmask the "real person" down inside.
Be creative rather than traditional. Look for new ways of reaching out and encouraging that person.
Be available rather than distant. Open your heart *and your home!*

APPREHENSION

But I do not consider my life of any account as dear to myself, in order that I may finish my course, and the ministry which I received from the Lord Jesus.
Acts 20:24 (NASB)

Apprehension is a notch or two above worry, but it feels like its twin. It's *not knowing what will happen to me.* Paul refused to run when apprehension whistled at him. Openly acknowledging its presence, he nevertheless stood his ground with the ringing words of Acts 20:24 (NASB).

THE CRIPPLING REALITY
OF APPREHENSION

*"Who of you by worrying can add
a single hour to his life?"*
Matthew 6:27

Apprehension. It's no sin, nor is it reason for embarrassment. It is, rather, proof positive that you're human. Unfortunately, it tends to smother your pleasant dreams by placing a pillow over your faith. Apprehension will strap a short leash on your vision and teach you to roll over and play dead when scary statistics and pessimistic reports snap their fingers.

DETERMINATION

... You have heard of Job's perseverance and have seen what the Lord finally brought about ...
James 5:11

Apprehension is impressive until determination pulls rank on it and forces it to salute. This is especially true when determination has been commissioned by the King of kings.

Come Aside And Over-Come Apprehension

I want to know Christ and the power of his resurrection and the fellowship of sharing in his sufferings, becoming like him in his death.
Philippians 3:10

We see Paul's determination expressed again in the familiar words of Philippians 3:7-15. Meditate on this passage, and be willing to ask God to show you anything you need for overcoming apprehension in your life.

How Honest Am I?

*Better a poor man whose walk is blameless
than a rich man whose ways are perverse.*
Proverbs 28:6

"Gentlemen: Enclosed you will find a check for $150. I cheated on my income tax return last year and have not been able to sleep ever since. If I still have trouble sleeping I will send you the rest. Sincerely ..."

THE WORST OF ALL FRAUDS

Save me, O Lord, from lying
lips and from deceitful tongues.
Psalm 120:2

To cheat oneself. Really, that lies at the heart of *every* human act of deception. Philip Bailey, the nineteenth-century poet, once made this stabbing statement: "The first and worst of all frauds is to cheat oneself. All sin is easy after that."

HOW ARE YOU SLEEPING

*My son, preserve sound
judgment and discernment ... when
you lie down, your sleep will be sweet.*
Proverbs 3:21, 24

Having a problem sleeping because you are uneasy about your dishonesty? Wonderful! You ought to be glad you can't sleep. It's the cheater who *sleeps* who's really got a problem worth losing sleep over!

COME ASIDE AND GROW IN INTEGRITY

But Zacchaeus stood up and said to the Lord, "Look, Lord! Here and now I give half of my possessions to the poor, and if I have cheated anybody out of anything, I will pay back four times the amount."
Luke 19:8

Learn everything you can from the example of Zacchaeus (in Luke 19:1-10) on how a man short on integrity finds it through Christ. In what ways might God want you to follow that man's example?

DECEMBER

KEEPING CONFIDENCES

*He who conceals his hatred has lying lips,
and whoever spreads slander is a fool.*
Proverbs 10:18

Our minds might be compared to a cemetery, filled with graves that refuse to be opened. Much information we hear, no matter how juicy or dry, must rest in peace in its coffin, sealed in silence beneath the epitaph: "Shared in confidence – kept in confidence."

Wise Counsel

When there are many words, transgression is unavoidable, but he who restrains his lips is wise.
Proverbs 10:19 (NASB)

He who goes about as a tale-bearer reveals secrets, but he who is trustworthy conceals a matter.
Proverbs 11:13 (NASB)

Do you restrain your lips? Are you verbally trustworthy?

Rules To Rule The Tongue

Likewise the tongue is a small part of the body, but it makes great boasts. Consider what a great forest is set on fire by a small spark.
James 3:5

1. **W**hatever you're told in confidence, *do not repeat*.
2. Whenever you're tempted to talk, *do not yield*.
3. Whenever you're discussing people, *do not gossip*.
4. However you're prone to disagree, *do not slander*.

Genuine Body Life

*Now we who are strong ought
to bear the weaknesses of those without
strength and not just please ourselves.*
Romans 15:1 (NASB)

We who are strong ought to bear the
weaknesses of those without strength.

WHAT'S THE DIFFERENCE?

"You shall not covet your neighbor's house. You shall not covet your neighbor's wife, or his manservant or maidservant, his ox or donkey, or anything that belongs to your neighbor."
Exodus 20:17

What *is* envy? How does it differ from its twin, jealousy? Envy wants to have what someone else possesses. Jealousy wants to possess what it already has. It was envy that sold Joseph into slavery, drove David into exile, threw Daniel in the den, and put Christ on trial.

The Remedy For Envy

No, in all these things we are more than conquerors through him who loved us.
Romans 8:37

Contentment. Feeling comfortable and secure with where you are and who you are. Not having to "be better" or "go further" or "own more" or "prove to the world" or "reach the top" or ...

You Are You

Do not neglect your gift ...
1 Timothy 4:14

Having some big struggles with envy? Eating your heart out because several others are a step or two ahead of you in the race and gaining momentum? *Relax.* You are *you* – not them! And you are responsible to do the best you can with what you've got for as long as you're able.

COME ASIDE AND
BE CONTENT

The Lord bless you and keep you;
the Lord make his face shine upon you
and be gracious to you; the Lord turn
his face toward you and give you peace.
Numbers 6:24-26

Think about the ingredients for contentment implied in this famous Hebrew blessing.

We Must Speak!

So faith comes from hearing,
and hearing by the word of Christ.
Romans 10:17 (NASB)

I can count on one hand the number of people in my entire life who have suddenly come up and asked me about Jesus Christ. While no one can discount the value of a godly life, that alone never brought any one into the family of God. "Faith," please remember, "comes from hearing ..."

IF YOU KNOW JESUS, YOU'VE GOT THE RIGHT ANSWER

"He went to him and bandaged his wounds, pouring on oil and wine. Then he put the man on his own donkey, took him to an inn and took care of him."
Luke 10:34

As you rub shoulders with hungry, thirsty humanity and sense their inner ache for help and hope, remember to speak of Jesus Christ ... But don't stop there. Remember the good Samaritan? He didn't merely give the wounded man a tract.

LOVE THAT ACTS

*But if someone who is supposed to
be a Christian has money enough
to live well, and sees a brother in
need, and won't help him –
how can God's love be within him?*
1 John 3:17 (TLB)

But if someone who is supposed to be a
Christian ... sees a brother in need, and
won't help him – how can God's love be
within him?

Make Time To Be Sensitive

Even a child is known by his actions,
by whether his conduct is pure and
right. Ears that hear and eyes that
see — the Lord has made them both.
Proverbs 20:11-12

Parental sensitivity rates desperately low these days. It's part of the fallout of our rapid pace. Solomon tells us that our children "make themselves known" by their deeds, their actions. He then reminds us that we have ears and eyes that ought to hear and see (*Proverbs 20:11-12*). Stop. Look. Listen.

PARENTING 101

*Fathers, do not embitter your children,
or they will become discouraged.*
Colossians 3:21

A basic task parents accept when they have children is to build the self-esteem and confidence of each child. Sensitive parents realize they need to be in tune with the thoughts and feelings of their children. They listen to clues they give and react appropriately. The sensitive heart rubs its fingers along the edges of another's life, feeling for the deep cracks ... the snags ... taking the time to hear ... to care ... to give ... to share.

COME ASIDE AND
GROW IN SENSITIVITY

"The day of the Lord is near for all nations.
As you have done, it will be done to you;
your deeds will return upon your own head."
Obadiah 15

God's hatred of human insensitivity resounds in Obadiah 10-15, in which the nation of Edom is condemned for its treatment of God's people during their distress. Get close to God's heart as you read these piercing words.

Don't Be Ignorant About Ignorance

*A fool finds no pleasure in understanding
but delights in airing his own opinions.*
Proverbs 18:2

Slice it any way you wish, ignorance is *not* bliss. Dress it in whatever garb you please, ignorance is *not* attractive. Neither is it the mark of humility nor the path to spirituality. It certainly is not the companion of wisdom. It is the breeding ground for fear, prejudice, and superstition.

THE LEGACY
OF LEARNING

*When the Lord finished speaking to
Moses on Mount Sinai, he gave him the
two tablets of the Testimony, the tablets of
stone inscribed by the finger of God.*
Exodus 31:18

Knowledge is not an enemy of the faith
but an ally. Trace your heritage back to
Moses and you find that the people were
given the truth of God in written form that
they might *know* and that their children
might *know* the right path to follow.

CALL THE GAME BY ITS CORRECT NAME

"Do not judge, and you will not be judged. Do not condemn, and you will not be condemned ..."
Luke 6:37

Let's label. That's a favorite parlor game among Christians. Any number can play. But it's especially appealing to those who are given to oversimplification and making categorical comments. The game really needs another name ... *Let's Judge*. When you play this game you're often setting yourself up as judge and jury, declaring information that is exaggerated or thirdhand or just plain untrue.

LABELS

But if you show favoritism, you sin and are convicted by the law as law-breakers.
James 2:9

Pasting labels on people and churches and schools with only partial facts, feelings, and opinions to back those statements up is worse than unfair ... it's downright unchristian.

THE POWER OF
THE TONGUE

*With the tongue we praise our Lord
and Father, and with it we curse men,
who have been made in God's likeness.*
James 3:9

Reckless words pierce like a sword, but
the tongue of the wise brings healing.
Proverbs 12:18

A Season To Draw Near

"For God so loved the world that he gave his one and only Son, that whoever believes in him shall not perish but have eternal life."
John 3:16

During this season of the year, it's important that we rivet into our heads exactly what we're celebrating. It is our Savior's arrival, not Santa's. The significance of giving presents is to be directly related to God's presenting us the gift of His Son – and our kiddos need that reminder year in and year out.

Economic Danger

A gift given in secret soothes anger, and a bribe concealed in the cloak pacifies great wrath.
Proverbs 21:14

Before every purchase, *think*. Ask yourself some direct, penetrating questions: Is this within my budget? Is it appropriate? Is it really saying what I want it to say? Gifts you *make* are often much more appreciated (and much less expensive) than those you buy.

IMPRESSING BUT NOT IMPARTING

To this you were called, because Christ suffered for you, leaving you an example, that you should follow in his steps.
1 Peter 2:21

We represent the King. We are His chosen ambassadors, doing His business "in season and out of season." Then let's do it *this* season! People are wide open to the gospel these days. Forget about trying to impress others by what you buy. Spend more time imparting what you already possess.

DECEMBER 23

GUARD YOURSELF

Do not get drunk on wine, which leads to debauchery. Instead, be filled with the Spirit.
Ephesians 5:18

One of the most effective maneuvers of the world system is to create a false sense of excitement. The Christian can get "high" very easily on the crest of the Christmas wave. But the cold that sweeps in on the tail of a fading afterglow can be a depressing experience. Guard yourself. Keep a firm hand on the controls. Don't be deceived. Enjoy the 25th ... but not at the expense of the 26th.

TAKE A SECOND LOOK

By the word of the Lord were
the heavens made, their starry
host by the breath of his mouth.
Psalm 33:6

When reading God's Word, you need to force yourself to observe, to take notice, to read like a detective examining the evidence, to discipline yourself to become saturated with the particulars of the passage. Such attention to detail will supply you with the raw materials you must have to interpret God's Word accurately.

Come Aside And See With New Eyes

The shepherds returned, glorifying and praising God for all the things they had heard and seen, which were just as they had been told.
Luke 2:20

Reflect on all your observations as you gaze on the scene at Bethlehem in Luke 2:1-20. Strain to see what you've never noticed before.

RENEW YOUR HOPE

But if we hope for what we do not yet have, we wait for it patiently.
Romans 8:25

The wrappings and ribbons are in the trash can. The manger scene is going back to the attic. The friends and family have said goodbye and now the house feels empty and so do you. Remember to keep this in mind: There is One who waits to fill your heart and renew your hope. He was there on December 24, and He's still with you on December 26.

BACKING OFF

There is a time for everything ...
Ecclesiastes 3:1

In the book of Ecclesiastes, Solomon, the wise, passes along to us a list of various types of "appointed time" on earth. Among them he mentions "a time to heal ... a time to shun embracing ... a time to give up as lost ... a time to be silent ..." I see in these words of counsel one strong undercurrent of advice: *Back off!* It is often wise to relax our intensity, refuse to force an issue, allow nature to take its course, "let sleeping dogs lie."

PATIENCE IS A VIRTUE

And so after waiting patiently,
Abraham received what was promised.
Hebrews 6:15

Waiting is as necessary as planting and fertilizing. When the time is right, things flow very naturally, very freely. To rush or force creates friction-scars that take years to erase. Like the little boy who plants the seed and then nervously digs it up every day to see if it is growing.

QUESTIONS

"Now I am going to him who sent me, yet none of you asks me, 'Where are you going?'"
John 16:5

Far too many sheep in the fold have turned a deaf ear to the questions of goats outside the gate. We are busily engaged in a mutual admiration campaign, complimenting one another's wool ... or gloating over our position in the pen. Most sheep have *stopped considering the questions* and have *started analyzing the answers.*

Put On Your Sunday Best: Your Armor

Be self-controlled and alert.
Your enemy the devil prowls
around like a roaring lion
looking for someone to devour.
1 Peter 5:8

Like a lion, our adversary prowls silently, camouflaged in the garb of our physical habits and our mental laziness, seeking to devour. At the precise moment we need the most, when it will have its greatest impact, he snatches away the very truth we need the most, leaving us with hardly a memory of what God said earlier. It occurs *every* Lord's Day in every language on every continent ... at every local church where the Scripture is declared.

CONSECRATE
THE NEW YEAR

*O Lord, truly I am your servant; I am
your servant, the son of your maidservant;
you have freed me from my chains.*
Psalm 116:16

When the new year becomes a reality at
midnight, give God your year afresh and
anew. Down deep – down in the depths of
your spirit – dedicate yourself to Him as
though for the first time in your life. Tell
him you are *His* and His *alone* ... and that
you want the new year to be His year for
you through and through.